THE SOUTHERN RAILWAY COLI

Kent and Susse:
Reflections

A Wainwright Class C locomotive, No 31216, in beautifully clean condition, shunts at Ashford Works on 21st April 1960.

The 5.19 p.m. Horsham to Brighton train approaches Christ's Hospital Station on 24th March 1961. The coaches are from Maunsell main line corridor set No. 952 which was built in 1936. The engine is Class E4, No. 32503 which was built at Brighton in 1900.

THE SOUTHERN RAILWAY COLLECTION

Kent and Sussex Reflections

Terry Gough

•RAILWAY HERITAGE•
from
The NOSTALGIA Collection

© Terry Gough 1984 and 2004

First published in 1984 as *The Southern in Kent and Sussex* by Oxford Publishing Company
New Silver Link Publishing edition first published in 2004

British Library Cataloguing in Publication Data

A catalogue record for this book is available from the British Library.

ISBN 1 85794 127 6

Silver Link Publishing Ltd
The Trundle
Ringstead Road
Great Addington
Kettering
Northants NN14 4BW

Tel/Fax: 01536 330588
email: sales@nostalgiacollection.com
Website: www.nostalgiacollection.com

Printed and bound in Great Britain

ABBREVIATIONS

BR	British Railways
GWR	Great Western Railway
KESR	Kent & East Sussex Railway
LBSCR	London, Brighton & South Coast Railway
LCDR	London, Chatham & Dover Railway
LMSR	London Midland & Scottish Railway
LSWR	London & South Western Railway
SECR	South Eastern & Chatham Railway
SER	South Eastern Railway
SR	Southern Railway

CONTENTS

A contrast in motive power at Paddock Wood on 20th August 1959. In the 'down' platform is Class H No. 31520 propelling two ex-LBSCR coaches on the 2.10p.m. Tonbridge to Maidstone West train. On the 'up' through line is Class N1 No. 31878, which has just brought in a freight train from the Maidstone line.

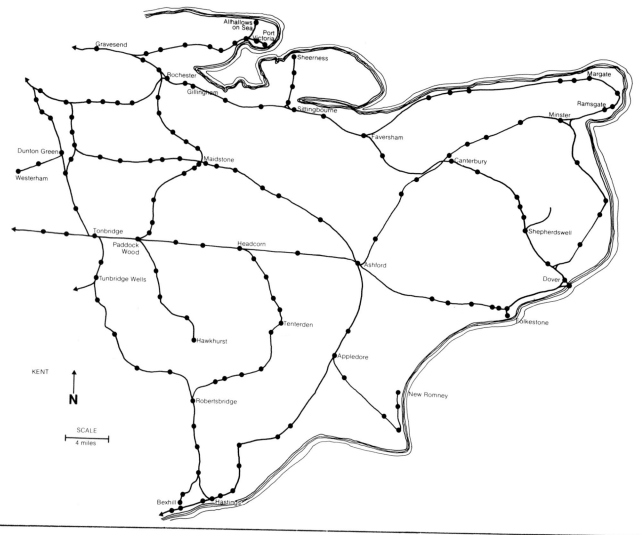

KENT

N

SCALE
4 miles

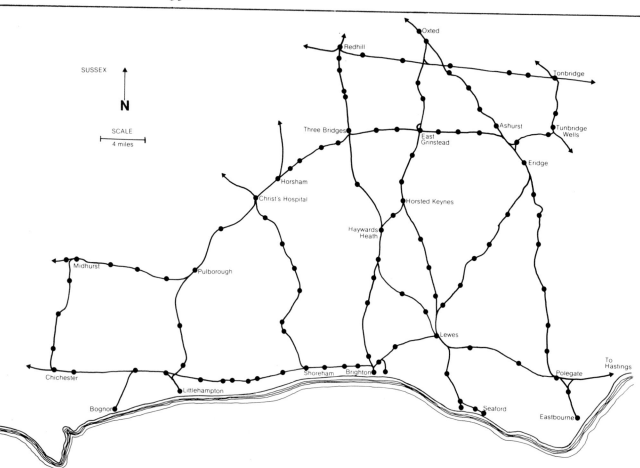

SUSSEX

N

SCALE
4 miles

THE RAILWAYS OF KENT AND SUSSEX
1955-1963

The railway systems in Kent and Sussex developed in complete contrast to each other. In Kent, the presence of both the London, Chatham & Dover Railway (LCDR) and the South Eastern Railway (SER) resulted in many of the major towns being served by both companies. Competition was so intense that duplication of routes almost brought about complete financial ruin, particularly to the former company.

A major prize for the companies was to capture the traffic of the Channel ports, and they both had main lines from London to Dover, the LCDR by way of North Kent and Canterbury and the SER, through Tonbridge, originally via Redhill but later direct through Sevenoaks. Both companies also sought the lucrative traffic which would accrue from the resorts of Margate and Ramsgate. The LCDR approached the Isle of Thanet along the North Kent Coast, and the SER by striking north-east from Ashford through Canterbury. The formation of the joint Committee, in 1899, known as the South Eastern & Chatham Railway, was a desperate attempt to come to terms with this situation. It was hoped that with the combined operation, solvency could be maintained, but the SECR itself was continually plagued with financial problems. Despite this duplication of effort, it is extraordinary that, to this day, very few of the lines in Kent have succumbed to closure. Indeed, during the period covered by this album, modernization dramatically improved the rail services throughout Kent. The unusual, and often unhelpful, pattern of services which was developed in the early days persisted through the Grouping. It survived nationalization, and was only eradicated when the main lines were electrified between 1959 and 1961. Not only was the frequency erratic, with no fixed interval service, but successive trains on a given line would not necessarily stop at the same intermediate stations. The intending passengers thus had to ensure whether the next train from their station of origin was calling at their destination. The previous train may well have done, in which case the next one would probably not be so obliging. So often modernization has meant rationalization; a euphemism for wholesale closure and a reduced service on the remaining lines. The electrification programme for Kent was ambitious and has been extremely successful. Since this book concerns, in the main, steam-operated services, a detailed description of the electrification programme is outside its scope, but, in brief, the main lines were electrified in two stages:

1) The North Kent line to Margate, Ramsgate and Dover via Canterbury East on 15th June 1959.

2) The Sevenoaks to Dover line on 12th June 1961, together with the Paddock Wood to Maidstone branch.

Of the secondary routes, the Dover to Ramsgate line was electrified in January 1961, followed by the Maidstone East to Ramsgate line via Ashford and Canterbury West on 9th October 1961.

The timetable of services in Kent changed substantially on electrification, but the map of the railways differs little today from that of the days of the SECR. The only route of substantial length closed prior to nationalization was the SER line from Canterbury West to Folkestone, but this passed through a thinly populated area and was, in any case, almost parallel to the LCDR main line from Canterbury East to Dover. This was duplication taken to extremes, so it was no wonder that one line was closed. The Southern Railway carried out significant modification to the system on the Isle of Thanet, which had become unwieldy through competition. Since nationalization, there have been no closures other than branch lines, although the Ashford to Hastings route has periodically been threatened. Early British Railways closures included Queenborough to Leysdown and Canterbury West to Whitstable Harbour, which, in any case, had been closed to passengers since 1931. During the period covered by this book, the Hoo Junction to Allhallows-on-Sea, Paddock Wood to Hawkhurst, Appledore to New Romney, Dunton Green to Westerham, and Crowhurst to Bexhill West branches have all been closed, at least to passenger services.

Mention must be made of two Colonel Stephens railways, the East Kent Railway and the Kent & East Sussex Railway, both of which became part of the Southern Region system. Both of these railways operated antiquated motive power and rolling stock which was usually obtained second-hand from other railways, including the Southern Railway and its predecessors. The East Kent Railway was closed to passengers in 1948, but a freight service was maintained on part of the system for many years afterwards. The Kent & East Sussex Railway was closed to regular services in 1954, but still saw occasional special workings thereafter. Although the northern part of the line, connecting the SER main line to Dover with Tenterden, has now been lifted, part of the remainder of the railway, which connected with the Hastings main line, is now a privately-operated steam railway.

Sussex was the stronghold of the London, Brighton & South Coast Railway (LBSCR), with an efficiently run and compact network of lines. The majority of lines ran from north to south, for the simple reason that most traffic was between London and the coastal resorts. There was, in addition, a route along the South Coast itself, all the way from Hastings in the east to Chichester, and into Hampshire to join the London & South Western Railway at Havant. There was also a line running east to west connecting Tunbridge Wells with Horsham, although there were no through services, and it was operated in segments. The LBSCR was forward-looking and, even in the early 1900s, much standardization of rolling stock was evident. The LBSCR was early in the application of electric traction, particularly in the London area where an electric service was established in 1909.

The Southern Railway, as part of its extensive modernization programme, introduced an electric train service from London to Brighton and Worthing in 1933, with six trains each way per hour, including one non-stop taking 60 minutes to Brighton. Two years later, electric services were extended to Hastings and Seaford, the latter on the line to Newhaven for the Dieppe ferry service. In 1938, the Mid-Sussex line, from Dorking North to Littlehampton, was electrified, together with the remainder of the South Coast line to Portsmouth. Further plans for electrification were shelved due to the outbreak of war and, indeed, the remaining lines, mostly in East Sussex, retained steam-operated services right up to closure or up to the introduction of diesels in the 1960s. Some lines were dieselized, only to be subsequently closed. Herein lies another difference between Kent and Sussex, for despite the superior standard of service in Sussex, many of these lines have suffered closure.

During the period covered by this book, the railway in East Sussex has virtually been destroyed, with major closures being Eridge to Polegate, Uckfield to Lewes and East Grinstead to Lewes. It is no longer possible to travel from Tunbridge Wells to Three Bridges, although East Grinstead still has a northbound service to London. Apart from the latter, none of these lines were branches, but were valuable cross-country routes connecting towns of considerable importance. Even the short electrified line between Horsted Keynes and Haywards Heath has been closed. To the west of the London to Brighton main line the situation is a little better and the Mid-Sussex route is still open. However, the two branches from Horsham, one to Guildford and the other to Brighton, have both gone. Although never very popular, in combination they offered a pleasant route to Brighton for passengers from Surrey. To reach Brighton nowadays, from, for example, the Guildford and Woking area, involves either a long journey via Portsmouth and along the South Coast, or into Waterloo and across to Victoria for the Brighton main line. All the railways to Midhurst have now been closed, but for many years trains were lightly-loaded and services were rather infrequent.

In conclusion, the railways of Kent, which began in such chaos, have not only survived, but have been modernized in the most acceptable sense of the word. The extensive network of the early days still survives. In Sussex, about half of the network has been closed, the major survivors being those lines that were electrified prior to World War II. This volume is an attempt to capture the railway scene in Kent and Sussex in the period prior to the last major changes. A small number of changes have been made since the first edition.

Terry Gough, Sherborne, 2004

Plate 1: Class L, No. 31764 at Sittingbourne with the 8.35a.m. from Victoria, on 12th March 1959. The train has split at Chatham, the front part being for Ramsgate and the rear half, seen here, for Dover. As an illustration of the peculiarity of the timetable, on the line between Rochester and Faversham, the first of several successive trains from Victoria stopped at all stations, except Rochester, Rainham, Newington and Teynham. The next train stopped at Rochester and Rainham, but not at Newington or Teynham. The following one omitted Rochester and Gillingham and the fourth train called at Teynham but not at the other stations. The Southern Railway concrete mile post declares that the engine is 44¾ miles from London, this referring to Victoria, although Charing Cross, by the most direct route, is two miles shorter. The train, just visible on the right, is the connecting service to Sheerness-on-Sea. This branch, which is 8 miles in length, was electrified three months after this photograph was taken, at the same time as the lines to Ramsgate and Dover. Prior to this, electric trains ran only from London to Gillingham, which was part of the Southern Railway's pre-war system.

Plate 2: Class 2MT, No. 41310 is seen with a one coach train at Faversham on 12th March 1959. During the period immediately prior to electrification, training of drivers for the new trains was undertaken with push-pull steam-hauled trains. One such train consisted of two ex-LBSCR coaches and the one in the platform is the former LSWR directors' saloon which was built in 1885. It was latterley used as an inspection coach by the Southern management. To see this unique vehicle, charging along the main line, was indeed an unexpected bonus for visitors to Kent, in the last months of main line steam.

Plate 3: From the days of the LCDR, provision of adequate motive power for the heavy North Kent trains has always caused a strain on resources. British Railways inherited a collection of ageing 4-4-0s of SECR origin, apart from the more modern and powerful 'Schools' and other Southern Railway-built locomotives. There was, however, insufficient modern motive power for all trains, and in the late 1950s it was necessary to allocate a number of the new standard express locomotives to Stewarts Lane, Their presence was short-lived and in only a few months, they were replaced by electric multiple units. Class 5MT. No. 73086 is captured just beyond Sittingbourne with the 9.35 a.m. Victoria to Ramsgate train. Unlike the previous train, there was no portion for Dover. To the left is the new signal box, in preparation for the introduction of colour light signals.

Plate 4: Faversham was the junction for the lines to Dover and Ramsgate. The Dover line was opened in 1860 to Canterbury, and the following year to Dover. The Ramsgate line, opened between 1860 and 1863, was regarded as less important, but, over the years, the situation has been reversed and this is now the main line. Dover is reached more rapidly via Tonbridge and the distance is one mile shorter. Some Dover trains originated at Faversham either by splitting the 'down' London train, or by connection. In this photograph of the 11.35 a.m. from Victoria approaching Faversham, the engine for the Dover train can be seen in the background. The Ramsgate train is hauled by the last member of the 'King Arthur' class, No. 30806, *Sir Galleron*. Despite the presence of two Pullman cars in this train, offering both first and third class accommodation for a supplementary fare, the train stops at all eleven stations between Sittingbourne and Ramsgate. Chestfield & Swalecliffe Halt was not so fortunate.

Plate 5: The North Kent resorts were very popular with Londoners and, at the height of the season, there were many extra trains, starting not only from Victoria, but also from stations in South East London, such as Blackheath. There was a procession of trains returning to London on Sunday evenings, rather like a small version of the rush hour. Scheduled trains left Ramsgate for the North Kent route approximately every 15 minutes between 4.40p.m. and 7.18p.m. In addition, there were excursion trains including some from other regions. On Sundays, during winter months, there were only four trains over the same period. Many of the weekend trains in summer were worked by Class N, 2-6-0s, which, during the week, were employed on heavy freight haulage. Class N, No. 31412, of Stewarts Lane Shed, with the 6.30p.m. Ramsgate to Victoria train, leaves Whitstable & Tankerton. Although this photograph was taken in August 1958, almost a year before electrification, the third rail is already in position.

Plate 6: Margate, with its seaside, amusement arcades, winkle stalls and other holiday paraphernalia, also had a modern station which was built by the Southern Railway. There were originally three stations at Margate, known as Margate West, Margate East (both LCDR) and Margate Sands, the terminus of the SER line from Ramsgate. In 1926, Margate West became the Southern Railway's new Margate Station and Margate Sands was closed. This was the result of simplifying the railways on Thanet to enable through workings without reversal, from Margate West to Ramsgate and thence to Dover. Margate East was not closed until 1953. At Margate, on 12th March 1959, the 1.50p.m. Ramsgate to Victoria working is headed by 'Schools' class No. 30919 *Harrow*. The first batch of 'Schools' class locomotives, built in 1930, were not fitted with smoke deflectors but these were added only a year later. The engines were built with chimneys of modest proportions, but larger diameter chimneys were fitted to several of the class by Bulleid, detracting a little from the overall pleasing appearance of these engines.

Plate 7: As part of the Thanet lines' re-organization in 1926 *(see Plate 6),* Ramsgate Station was resited. Both of the pre-grouping stations, which were termini, were closed and the LCDR station was converted into an amusement hall. The new station was for through working, and had parallel carriage sheds and a sizeable motive power depot. On a winter's evening in 1959, a rebuilt 'West Country' class, No. 34017, *Ilfracombe* virtually blots out the already weak sun, when pulling away from Ramsgate with the 5.02 p.m. to Victoria. The combined efforts of 'King Arthur' class No. 30806, and several engines on shed in the background, further darken the sky. A memorable and impressive sight, but casting a melancholy feeling over the observer, knowing that, within a few months, all steam engines will be banned from the area. Their replacements will be quiet, sleek and clean.

Plate 8: The Southern Railway installed a number of massive ferro-concrete coaling stages at the larger depots, including Ramsgate. The water column is also of Southern Railway origin and, indeed, there is nothing in this photograph to indicate that the railways reached the Ramsgate area before Grouping. The wagons in the background are modern, and the two engines were built in 1932 and 1953. In the foreground is 'Schools' class, No. 30930, *Radley* and behind is Standard class 2MT, No. 84021. The latter type of engine, which was built at Derby, was used on the local services throughout East Kent, and several were allocated to Ramsgate Shed.

Plate 9: Desolation. A once elegant Wainwright Class D express passenger engine, relegated to carriage heating duties at Ramsgate. The engine has even been converted to a 4-2-0, although this is hardly likely to influence the performance of its current duties. It seems, too, to be sinking into the ground in shame. The engine is No. 31501, which was withdrawn in 1953, six years before the photograph was taken. It was cut up a few months later. It had replaced an engine of even greater age, a Class 0 which had undertaken the same task since 1929.

Plate 10: The LCDR shed at Gillingham was used right up until electrification, although it was demolished thereafter. It was a dark and rather cramped building, with three roads, and was situated just east of Gillingham Station. In early BR days, it had an allocation of about 50 locomotives, the vast majority of these being the Class C goods engines which were designed by Wainwright for the SECR. The allocation was substantially reduced by the time this photograph was taken in February 1958, but the C class is still in evidence with Nos. 31510 and 31682 in view. These engines were used on the North Kent freight trains, and also on local passenger services within the Medway towns area, and on the Sheerness branch. There were also a few H class 0-4-4Ts to work Sheerness and Allhallows trains. Several 4-4-0 tender engines were available for semi-fast passenger work (see Plate 1).

Plate 11 (top right): Shepherdswell Station, on the Faversham to Dover LCDR route, was the junction for the freight only line to Tilmanstone Colliery. This was all that remained of the former East Kent Railway, which was built from 1911, predominantly to serve the numerous collieries in the area. Its secondary objective was to carry agricultural produce, but passengers were always regarded as incidental. Beyond Tilmanstone, there were several smaller collieries, but many of these closed in 1914. However the line remained open to Eastry and Wingham collieries and a passenger service commenced in 1916. It was planned to extend this line to join the Ashford to Ramsgate line near Canterbury but, by 1925, the East Kent Railway had only managed to get 1¼ miles beyond Wingham. The plans were abandoned, and the terminus became known as Canterbury Road. The development of Richborough as a port, during World War I, encouraged the East Kent Railway to extend in this direction, but only for freight traffic. However, in 1925, a passenger service was also introduced on this section, but it only ran as far as Sandwich Road. Traffic was always light beyond Tilmanstone, and shortly after nationalization, all passenger services were withdrawn. Motive power has always been other people's cast-offs, and ex-SECR Stirling Class 0 locomotives purchased from the Southern Railway have been the most common. The first, No. 372, was obtained in 1923 and remained on the East Kent Railway until 1949. In the intervening period it was rebuilt with an O1 boiler. Another Class 0 was obtained in 1928 (No. 376), but was sold six years later. Two O1s, the Wainwright rebuilds of the Class 0, were later purchased, No. 371 being scrapped in 1949 and No. 383 in 1951. However, this was not the end of this class as the mainstay of motive power, as British Railways allocated three of their own stock from Dover, to Tilmanstone Colliery trains. The photograph shows one of these, No. 31065, with a coal train at Shepherdswell on 21st April 1960. In contrast, on the right, is a Class 2 diesel, No. D5002 with a Dover-bound freight train. The overhead wires in the yard were installed so that shunting by electric locomotives could be performed, without the potential hazard of third rail pick-up.

Plate 12 (bottom right): Another contrast, with Class 01, No. 31258 shunting at Shepherdswell, and a new electric unit, No. 7144 leaving for Faversham. The electric service had begun almost a year before this photograph was taken.

Plate 14 *(below)*: Tonbridge was a railway centre of considerable interest and activity. The station and its surroundings were not particularly attractive, but the junctions at both the east and west ends of the station ensured a considerable variety of traffic. The original SER main line from London reached Dover from Redhill, but this was superseded by the more direct and hilly route through Sevenoaks, which is the present main line. The Redhill line became a cross-country route. The junction for the Hastings line was at the other end of the station, and in this 'vee' was situated the motive power depot *(see Plate 17)*. The author recalls his first visit to Tonbridge, and being dumbfounded by the fact that a place of such importance was not part of the Southern electric system. The Kent electrification plans were not announced for another seven years. Apart from the procession of expresses hauled mainly by 'Schools' and 'West Country' classes, during early September each year, there were, in addition, the hop-pickers' specials from London which passed through on their way to destinations such as Marden and Hawkhurst. Class C, No. 31693 is seen during the 1960 season on a special from London Bridge, with Maunsell set No. 466. By this time, the conductor rail had been laid, pending electrification during the following summer. Hop-pickers' and friends' trains were easily recognizable, as they usually carried a train number prefixed 'H', in addition to the standard disc route indicator.

Plate 13 *(above)*: Shunting a few wagons at Shepherdswell (East Kent Railway) Station, prior to taking empties to Tilmanstone Colliery, is No. 31258.

TONBRIDGE TO DOVER

Plate 15: Although hop-pickers' trains were not for use by ordinary ticket holders, it was an accepted practice to travel on them if seats were available. In general, they were rather slow, and regular trains were, of course, given preference. A returning special is seen at Tonbridge on the evening of 13th September 1959, hauled by Class C, No. 31293. This train was non-stop to London Bridge, but was routed via Redhill, thus making the journey even longer.

Plate 16: Tonbridge was the starting point for services to Maidstone. For many years this was operated by push-pull trains with SECR Class H tank engines, but occasionally newer stock was used. The photograph, taken on 19th May 1961, shows No. 31305 with a new BR standard corridor set No. 550, more than adequate for the branch. The water column in the foreground is of SECR pattern.

Plate 17 (above): The original shed at Tonbridge, built by the SER, was extensively modified by the SER and, much later, by the Southern Railway and yet again by BR. It was responsible for providing motive power for the main line stopping services, some of the Hastings and Redhill trains and the H class engines for the Maidstone, Westerham and Hawkhurst branches. As with Gillingham, there was an allocation of C class 0-6-0s and various 4-4-0s. In addition there were several Class N Moguls, and the Bulleid Q1s, for heavy freight operation. The roads at the rear of the shed were used as a dump for withdrawn engines. The shed was run down in the period leading up to the Kent electrification, increasingly so as Class 2 diesels became more numerous. The shed was closed in 1964 and demolished, although the site is still used to service diesel locomotives. Amongst the cinders and general grime at the front of the shed on 4th February 1958 is Class D1, No. 31492, being prepared to work a Tonbridge to Redhill passenger train.

Plate 18 (left) Paddock Wood was the first station on the main line east of Tonbridge and was the junction for Maidstone and Hawkhurst. The bay platform on the right was used for the occasional Maidstone train which started here. There were four through lines, the two centre ones having no platform faces, and being used by the expresses for Dover and London. Although Paddock Wood itself was little more than a village, the station was very active. It was situated in the heart of hop growing country and on 18th September 1960, a Tonbridge to Headcorn hop pickers' special pauses in the 'down' loop. The engine unusually working tender first is Class U1, No. 31906, and the passenger stock consists of a four coach Maunsell set, No 182.

Plate 19: The Hawkhurst branch curved away to the south, just beyond Paddock Wood Station, and this was an ideal point at which to observe main line trains, pounding along from Dover, on their way to London. It was the summit of a short climb at 1 in 220. The line between Tonbridge and Ashford was a fairly gentle grade in contrast to the line nearer London. It was also a virtually perfect straight line all the way between these two points. In addition to regular passenger trains, there were boat trains from both Dover and Folkestone. Here, 'West Country' class No. 34100 *Appledore* is seen with the 2.25 p.m. Dover Marine to Victoria train on 20th August 1959.

Plate 20: In 1958, the author decided to take a spring break, in Kent. The county has always suffered from heavier snowfalls than the rest of the South of England, but no one would expect snow in early April. Falls during the previous few days had been sufficiently heavy to block the Hawkhurst branch for a while. This photograph, taken on the SER main line at Headcorn, shows Class C, No. 31272 with a coal train to Tonbridge. Headcorn was the junction for the northern terminus of the Kent & East Sussex Railway, which had been closed four years previously *(see Plates 48 and 49)*.

Plate 21: Ashford was both an important railway junction and the operating hedquarters of the SECR. Ashford had grown from a village to a large town, as a direct result of the presence of the railway, with a carriage and wagon works, the locomotive works and a large motive power depot. The fortunes of the town were, therefore, in every sense, linked to the growth of the railway. From Ashford, there were trains to Hastings, with connections to all the South Coast resorts. Trains for the New Romney branch also started from Ashford. There was a direct line to Ramsgate, which was built by the SER, and reached Canterbury, 14 years before the LCDR, from Faversham. However, the LCDR encroached upon Ashford by extending its line from Maidstone, in 1884. The importance of Ashford as a junction has been maintained right up to the present day, and all lines radiating from here are still open. The works have, however, been drastically run down and are under threat of closure. The motive power depot has also gone, but there is a maintenance depot for electric units. On 3rd April 1956, 'King Arthur' class, No. 30804, *Sir Cador of Cornwall* is seen with the 10.12a.m. (all stations) from Tonbridge. This train terminates at Ashford, although there is a connecting service from Maidstone which runs on to Dover. It was unusual for a locomotive as large as a 'King Arthur' to work the local services, which were usually entrusted to the older 4-4-0s.

Plate 22: For many years, almost all short-haul freight trains were in the hands of Wainwright Class C engines. Here, No. 31255 trundles through Ashford, in April 1960, on an 'up' freight consisting of a few open wagons, a container wagon and a Southern Railway brake van. The works and shed were both some distance from the station, beyond the gantry in the background. The former lay to the right, and the latter to the left of the main line.

Plate 23: Not only a threat to the railway, but also to British car manufacturers. A train load of imported cars is being taken from Dover to London via Maidstone by Class N, No. 31875, on 21st April 1960. The lines in the foreground run into the locomotive works. To the left of the train are the extensive marshalling yards.

Plate 24: There were three stations at Folkestone, one to serve the town, one at the junction on the main line for the Harbour branch, and one at the Harbour itself for the cross-Channel ferries. Naming of stations in the Folkestone area has a rather complicated history. Folkestone Central was originally called Cheriton Arch and later Radnor Park. The junction station changed names six times before the turn of the century, and then remained Folkestone East until 1962, when it became Folkestone Junction. It was closed in 1965, although the line to the Harbour is still open for boat trains. The Harbour Station has always been known simply as Folkestone Harbour. There was also a station at Shorncliffe, opened as Shorncliffe Camp, which changed names four times before becoming Folkestone West in 1962. 'Schools' class, No. 30935, *Sevenoaks* is shown on a 'down' extra train from London Bridge to Dover, on the Easter weekend of 1959, at Folkestone Junction.

Plate 25: A dismal day at Folkestone Junction in March 1959, with 'King Arthur' class, No. 30798, *Sir Hectimere* hauling the 11.45 a.m. Dover Priory to Maidstone East train. The Harbour branch is to the right. The GWR pannier tank engine at the coaling stage was one of several of these engines used for banking and hauling the boat trains from the Harbour Station. The line is a little under ¾ mile long, and rises at an incline of 1 in 30 for much of the way to the main line.

Plate 26: A visit to Folkestone Junction a week later produced much better weather, and found 'Battle of Britain' class, No. 34067 *Tangmere* emerging into the sunlight from Martello Tunnel. The train is an empty carriage working from Dover, to form the 1.20 p.m. 'up' boat train from the Harbour to London. The Pacific locomotive will remain at the junction, whilst the stock is transferred to the Harbour and back by three pannier tanks. The sidings in the foreground are for storing boat train stock, and to enable the trains to reverse without congesting the main line. There are three tunnels between Folkestone and Dover, and it is at the other end of Martello Tunnel that yet another Folkestone station was situated. It was officially known as Warren Halt, but in the early British Railways timetables, at least, it was given the grand prefix of Folkestone.

Plate 27: A boat train in full cry, with 'Merchant Navy' class, appropriately No. 35001, *Channel Packet*. The train is leaving Folkestone Central on 26th March 1959. All the 'Merchant Navy' class locomotives were rebuilt by British Railways. The streamlined casing, whilst giving rise to a locomotive of most attractive lines, was a hindrance to maintenance, particularly with the several unconventional design features of Bulleid locomotives. The most obvious result of rebuilding was, of course, the loss of the streamlining. This revealed an engine of more conventional appearance, but the real advantage lay in the significantly increased reliability, and cheaper maintenance costs of the rebuilt engines. No. 35001 was rebuilt only a few months after this photograph was taken, and was one of the last of the class to be tackled. It was withdrawn in 1964, after covering over one million miles. Two of the class still exist, one in working order and the other on static display in the National Railway Museum.

Plate 28:   Ashford Locomotive Works was built by the SER in 1853. The LCDR had its Longhedge Works at Battersea in South London. Under Wainwright as Locomotive & Carriage Superintendent of the SECR, Longhedge Works was closed, and the maintenance and building of all SECR locomotives was carried out at Ashford. A view of the erecting shops, on 3rd April 1956, shows a variety of motive power under repair. To the left is a W class 2-6-4T goods engine, which was designed by Maunsell, and built in 1931. Behind this locomotive is an ex-LMSR 2-6-4T, and at the end of the line is a Maunsell Mogul. On the right are more SECR engines, a Class E1 express passenger 4-4-0, an H class 0-4-4 tank engine, and more 4-4-0s.

Plate 29:   Heavy repairs were still being undertaken in 1960, although by this time most of the older SECR locomotives had been scrapped rather than given general overhauls. However, Moguls, such as Class U1, No. 31909, were still much in evidence. All locomotives of this class, except the first member, which was converted from a K1 class tank engine, were built at Eastleigh, despite being based on an SECR design.

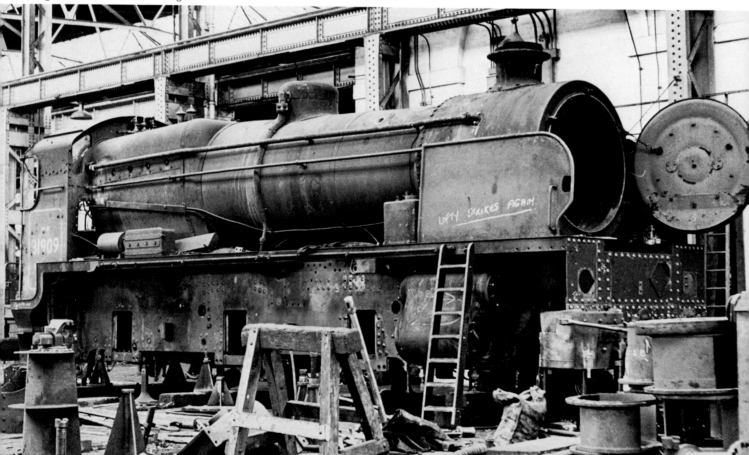

Plate 30: Outside the works, the signs were less encouraging as the scrap road inevitably contained a few worn out engines, usually, but not exclusively, of SECR origin. Class R1, No. 31337, was built as Class R in 1888, rebuilt in 1922, and withdrawn in February 1960. It is seen at Ashford two months after withdrawal, at this stage having lost only its numberplate. This was one of the engines which worked the Folkestone Harbour branch from 1944 until displacement, in 1959, by GWR tank engines *(see Plate 25)*.

Plate 31: Surplus to requirements. A line of 4-4-0s, displaced by the first stage of the Kent electrification, in store at Ashford Works on 21st April 1960. The engines are all Class L1, Nos. 31785, 31788 and 31784. The headcode on the first of the line optimistically shows Victoria to Dover. These engines were not rebuilds of Class L, although they were developed from them. They were built by the North British Locomotive Company for the Southern Railway in 1926. Although the engines in the photograph were cut up at Ashford, some members of the class were transferred to the Western Section and were used for a few months on empty stock and vans trains.

Plate 32: Ashford Motive Power Depot was the largest in Kent, the present shed being built by the Southern Railway in 1931. For many years it had an allocation of between 50 and 60 engines. There were substantial numbers of Class C and Class Q1 locomotives for freight work, mixed traffic 2-6-0s, and the 'Schools' and 'King Arthur' classes for express passenger trains. There were, of course, 4-4-0s for lesser passenger trains on the main line, and the H class locomotives for New Romney services. On 30th August 1955, the following engines were outside the shed; from left to right, Class C, No. 31059, Class U1, No. 31906, Class C, No. 31244, Class C2X, No. 32534, Class L1, No. 31754, Class E1, No. 31497, Standard class 4MT, No. 76059, Class E4, No. 32467, LMSR 2MT, No. 41316 and Class N1, No. 31822. The Class C2X locomotive is ex-works, and is en route to its home shed of Three Bridges.

Plate 33: Ashford Shed on 25th February 1962, with 'Schools' class No. 30926, *Repton* and Class C, No. 31218. By this time, all passenger trains were either electric or diesel-operated. The snowplough was a warning of things to come, as later in the day a blizzard struck Kent and lasted for several hours. The 'Schools' is beautifully clean, and was being prepared to work a special train.

Plate 34 (top right): The LCDR reached Maidstone in 1874, by constructing a line from Otford on the Sevenoaks branch. The line was extended to Ashford ten years later, and LCDR trains used their own small terminus just north of the SER station. Opposition from the SER to the scheme was strong, which was hardly surprising in view of its own well-established activities at Ashford. The terminus at Ashford closed in 1899, and all trains then used the through station, which, at the same time, became one of the Joint Committee's assets. The first section of the line, to Maidstone East, was electrified in 1939, but steam services continued to operate on to Ashford until October 1961, when this section was also electrified. In the years immediately prior to electrification, modern motive power and stock was almost exclusively employed, and was usually Standard 2-6-4Ts and BR Mk.1 coaches. On 28th March 1961, the 6.09 p.m. from Ashford is seen at Maidstone East. The engine, 4MT, No. 80038, is taking water prior to running round and returning to Ashford, bunker first. On the right is the connecting electric train to Victoria.

Plate 35 (bottom right): Most of the trains originating at Maidstone East continued beyond Ashford, either on the old SER line through Canterbury to Ramsgate, or down the main line to Dover. The 1.45 p.m. from Maidstone East took the latter route, and is hauled by Class 4MT, No. 80087 on 28th March 1961. The station, which has just had a footbridge installed, pending the introduction of the electric service, is Hollingbourne, 7½ miles beyond Maidstone.

Plate 36: A welcome change, in the form of Class N, No. 31868 and Bulleid set, No. 92. The train is the 5.58 p.m. Maidstone East to Margate, and is seen leaving Charing on 21st April 1960.

Plate 37: Shunting at Lenham, on 28th March 1961, is Class Q1, No 33033. The Q1s were built during World War II to a Bulleid design, and although devoid of any pretence of elegance, they were functional. They were the most powerful 0-6-0s on the railways of Britain. Building was shared between Ashford and Brighton, although the boilers all came from Eastleigh. The entire class was withdrawn between 1963 and 1966, although No. 33001 is now preserved.

Plate 38: The 3.25 p.m. train from Maidstone East at Ashford en route to Ramsgate on 21st April 1960. The engine is an ex-LMSR Ivatt 2-6-2 tank, No. 41311. These engines, and the more powerful 2-6-4Ts of Stanier design, were found on secondary services both in Kent and Sussex pending arrival of BR Standard tank engines.

Plate 39: BR Standard 2-6-2T, No. 84021 approaches Minster Junction from Margate with the 4.25 p.m. to Ashford, with Maunsell set No. 224 (first three coaches only). Minster was at the apex of a triangle, with lines approaching from Dover, Margate and Ashford.

Plate 40: Through trains from other regions reached Margate via Minster. The usual route from the Midlands was to pick up the SECR line at Reading, and approach the Isle of Thanet by way of Guildford, Tonbridge and Ashford. 'Schools' class, No. 30932, *Blundells* is seen, on 25th August 1960, operating with the 10.40a.m. from Wolverhampton. The bay on the left is for the local train to Dover. It was possible to travel from Ashford on a Margate train to Minster, change for Dover, and change again at Dover to return to the starting point, without reversing direction of travel.

Plate 41: The remaining line radiating from Ashford was that to Hastings, Bopeep Junction, which was opened by the SER in 1851. A branch was subsequently built by the SER to Dungeness and New Romney, leaving the Hastings line 8½ miles from Ashford, at Appledore. Both the Hastings and branch trains usually started from Ashford, the former being worked by 4-4-0 tender engines, and the latter by H class push-pull fitted tank engines. Patronage on both routes had been rather poor for a long time, partly because the lines traversed the thinly-populated area of Romney Marsh. Dungeness closed to passengers in 1937 but, at the same time, the New Romney line was relocated nearer the coast, with the provision of additional stations. Neither line featured in the Kent electrification scheme, but following elimination of all steam services in Kent, they were worked by diesel multiple units. The New Romney branch was closed to passengers in 1967, but the Hastings line has, after substantial operating economies, managed to survive, and is still worked by diesel units. Class H, No. 31310 is seen at Appledore with the 12.47p.m. Ashford to New Romney train on 3rd June 1958.

ASHFORD TO HASTINGS AND NEW ROMNEY

Plate 42 (right): Many years after the last steam train had left, Ham Street & Orlestone Station still retains reminders of earlier years. The station nameboard posts are made from old rails, with a standard Southern Railway green enamel board. The oil lamp is of original SECR pattern, complete with the name 'Ham Street' etched in blue on the lamp glass.

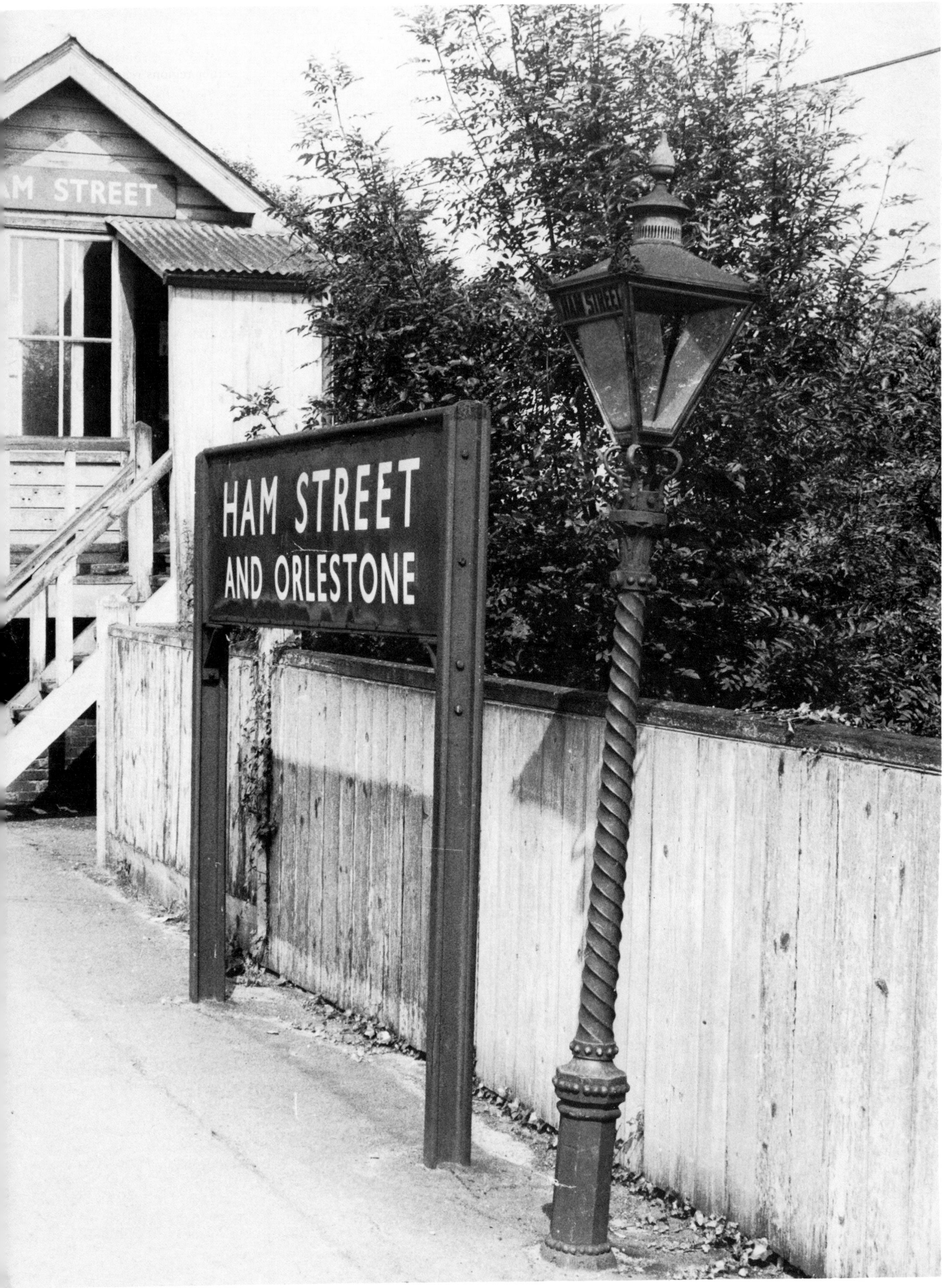
AM STREET
HAM STREET
AND ORLESTONE

Plate 43: Out of the eight stations between Ashford and Hastings, three were halts which were opened in 1907. Not all trains stopped at the halts. In 1953, Doleham Halt was served by six trains each way per day, plus one by request to the guard. There was no Sunday service. In 1965 the number had miraculously increased to a total of seventeen with almost as many on Sundays, but Snailham Halt had been closed. An hourly service has been maintained to the present day. The last ¾ mile into Hastings was electrified in 1935 as part of the Sussex electrification scheme. An electric train depot was provided at Ore for trains running from the Central Section.

Plate 44: The main line from Tonbridge to Hastings was opened by the SER in sections; to Tunbridge Wells in 1845, Robertsbridge in 1851, and to Battle and Hastings the following year. There were several narrow bore tunnels on the line, the one at Mountfield being of particularly mean proportions. As a result there has always been severe loading gauge restrictions on the Hastings line and the Southern Railway was obliged to build special narrow-bodied coaches. The line curves away sharply at Tonbridge, and climbs steeply with a maximum gradient of 1 in 53. Class C, No. 31280 is seen leaving Tonbridge with a Hastings-bound freight train on 4th February 1958.

TONBRIDGE TO HASTINGS

Plate 45 (top right): The first station situated south of Tonbridge was Southborough, but this was not built until 1893. It was renamed High Brooms in 1925. 'Schools' class, No. 30902, *Wellington* is shown on the 3.19p.m. Tonbridge to Hastings on 2nd May 1958. The restricted tunnel clearances also severely limited the types of engine which could be used, and fast trains were almost solely hauled by 'Schools' class locomotives. Lesser trains were usually powered by SECR 4-4-0s, and freight trains by Class C engines. The 'Schools' were popular and reliable engines, and although being 4-4-0s, were able to handle the heaviest expresses between London and Hastings. The author recalls, many years ago, staring in disbelief at a 'Schools' class engine at Tonbridge, and realizing that it really did only have four driving wheels.

Plate 46 (bottom right): Crowhurst was only five miles from Hastings, and was the junction for a short line to Bexhill-on-Sea, known, after the Grouping, as Bexhill West. There was a frequent service from Crowhurst to Bexhill West connecting with main line trains. On 3rd June 1958, 'Schools' class, No. 30937, *Epsom* with the 8.20a.m. from Charing Cross, produces few passengers for the branch. The branch push-pull sets are Nos. 660 and 661, each operated by an H class engine.

Plate 48 (below): Rolvenden was the headquarters of the KESR, with an engine shed and workshops. In the same manner as the East Kent Railway *(see Plate 11)*, motive power was normally obtained second-hand. The southern part of the line had several weak bridges, and nothing heavier than a 'Brighton Terrier' was normally used. The Rother Valley Railway had purchased No. 70 from the London, Brighton & South Coast Railway in 1901 and No. 71 in 1905. The former was taken into BR stock in 1948, and is now owned by the present operators of the KESR. No. 71 was less fortunate, and was scrapped in 1938. Upon nationalization, British Railways provided the same class of engine for the services, and these were allocated to St. Leonards. The northern part of the line was operated by an ex-LSWR saddleback, No. 335, and two LSWR 'Ilfracombe' goods engines, Nos. 282 and 284. All were scrapped by the time nationalization came, after which SECR Class 01 tender engines were used. The author made a trip on the last day of passenger services, 2nd January 1954, a bitterly cold and dull day. Closures in those days did not attract the attention that occurred in the succession of closures in the 1960s. It was not necessary to run extra-long trains, as happened, for example, on the Westerham branch *(see Plate 73)*. The last train to Robertsbridge left Tenterden at 4.15p.m., with only a handful of passengers, mostly local people. It was an uneventful but, nevertheless, memorable journey taking about 1 hour to cover 12½ miles. Long after closure, 'Terriers' were still seen on the southern half of the line and, for long trains, instead of double-heading which would exceed the weight limit, one engine was coupled at each end of the train. On 18th October 1959, Class A1 No. DS680 takes water at Rolvenden which, at this time, was hardly recognizable, with the works and even the station demolished. However, better things were in store for this part of the line, which is now in private hands and is open, for passenger traffic, between Tenterden and Bodiam.

KENT & EAST SUSSEX RAILWAY

Plate 47 (left): "Schools' class, No. 30939, *Leatherhead* with the 5.08p.m. Hastings to Charing Cross train, approaches Crowhurst on 3rd June 1958. The branch train is hiding on the right. Diesel multiple units had been introduced on the Hastings to London services during the previous year, and all trains were diesel-operated shortly after this photograph was taken. The diesel units, which were built at Eastleigh, had to have narrow slab-sided bodies, giving them a rather austere appearance. Although now virtually life-expired, they are still used on this line due to the high cost of providing specially designed replacements. The shuttle service to Bexhill West was also diesel-operated from 1958 but, because there were no tunnels, was able to use more conventional 'Hampshire' type units. The branch was closed with the introduction of the summer 1964 timetable.

Plate 49: Robertsbridge was a little over half way between Tonbridge and Hastings, and although never having the suffix 'Junction', it was, in fact, the junction for the Kent & East Sussex Railway (KESR). A bay was provided at the SECR station for branch trains. The branch was opened in 1900 to Rolvenden and was known as the Rother Valley Railway which accurately described its route. The station at Rolvenden was actually called Tenterden, for a short while, although the town was situated about two miles away. Such was the case with most of the stations, particularly on the northern extension to Headcorn, which was opened in 1905. The name of the railway was also changed, to the all-embracing Kent & East Sussex Railway, indicating to the unsuspecting traveller that there was, perhaps, a vast network of lines covering the two counties. There was another reason for a junction at Robertsbridge, and that was to reach a local flour mill, where freight traffic continued to be generated years after the KESR proper had lost its service. The mill even had its own locomotive, latterley an ex-SECR Class P 0-6-0T, which is now preserved. The KESR probably saw more passengers after closure than at most other times in its history. The age of the railway enthusiasts' special had arrived and, coupled with seasonal excursions for hop-picking, generated great activity on several days of the year. One such special is seen leaving Robertsbridge on 11th June 1961, double-headed by Classes D1, No. 31749 and L1, No. 31786, with a rake of SECR-style coaches.

Plate 51: There were two engines sheds in the Hastings area, one for the SER and the other, at St. Leonards, for the LBSCR. In conjunction with improvements made by the Southern Railway to facilities at Hastings, the station was rebuilt. To make way for this, the ex-SECR shed was closed in 1929. The entire stock was sent to the ex-LBSCR shed, which then had to provide motive power for the Hastings to London main line trains, the coast line, and other ex-LBSCR lines in the area. When electrification reached Hastings, the allocation was reduced. There were no more significant changes until the advent of diesels on the main line. Their arrival spelt the end for St. Leonards Shed, which closed in 1958. Outside the shed, on 14th August 1956, is Class L, No. 31762, ready to work a semi-fast to Tonbridge, and two Q1s, Nos. 33032 and 33039.

Plate 50: Another special which had visited Tenterden, appropriately named the 'Rother Valley Limited'. The engines are both 'Terriers', Nos. 32678 and DS377 and are seen at Crowhurst on 19th October 1958 en route for Hastings. No. DS377 was formerly Southern Railway No. 2635 and was the Brighton Works shunter. In 1947, it was repainted in Stroudley yellow, a livery which it still had when this photograph was taken. It was returned to general stock in 1959 as No. 32635, but retained the legend *Brighton Works* on the tanks. It was withdrawn in 1963. No. 32678 was withdrawn the same year, and was sold to Butlins.

TONBRIDGE TO REDHILL

Plate 52: A line of considerable importance ran due west from Tonbridge, and by passing through both LBSCR and LSWR territory, reached Reading. Only the short section as far as Edenbridge was in Kent, the majority of the line running through Surrey. The section to Redhill was the original SER main line from London, but even after losing this status, the line retained its value because of its connection to Reading and beyond. Until the advent of dieselization, Moguls handled the majority of trains. Present day passenger services are operated by diesel multiple units, and occasional locomotive-hauled trains. Apart from Leigh Halt, Penshurst was the first station out of Tonbridge. Penshurst had a typical SECR country signal box, which was situated between the 'up' and 'down' platforms which were end-on. The box was on the 'down' (i.e. Tonbridge-bound) side.

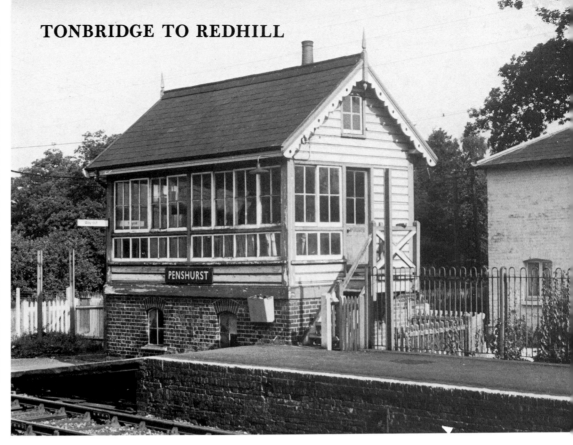

Plate 53: Class N, No. 31848 of Ashford Shed, prepares to leave Penshurst with the 11.38 a.m. Tonbridge to Redhill train on 19th May 1961. In the station yard is a crane with a wooden jib, typical of those seen throughout the South of England.

Plate 55: The SER reached Maidstone in 1844, following the valley of the River Medway from Paddock Wood. Prior to this Paddock Wood was call Maidstone Road. The LCDR did not reach Maidstone for another thirty years, but, by this time, the SER had long since connected Maidstone with North Kentwell. The Southern Railway must have regarded Maidstone as the end of the world, as both Maidstone stations were the terminal points of the pre-war electrification scheme from London. Maidstone West to Paddock Wood was electrified in 1961 and, prior to this, trains were usually push-pull operated. When the line opened, there were four intermediate stations, although the one located at Tovil, half a mile from Maidstone, was closed in 1943. The first station from Paddock Wood was Yalding, and Class H No. 31305 is seen here on 10th June 1961, on the 10.32a.m. from Tonbridge. The stock is BR-built push-pull set No. 616, originally Maunsell main line corridor coaches.

Plate 54: Pounding along between Leigh and Penshurst is an Ashford to Redhill freight train, hauled by Class N1 No 31879.

PADDOCK WOOD TO MAIDSTONE WEST

Plate 56: Another view of the station at Yalding, with the same engine, more than a year earlier, with the 5.20 p.m. Maidstone West to Tonbridge. The train is unusually long, and it is assumed that the working included empty carriages for Tonbridge.

Plate 57: In 1909, halts were opened at Beltring & Branbridges, two miles from Paddock Wood, and at Teston Crossing at the other end of the line. On 18th September 1960, Class H, No. 31518 enters Beltring & Branbridges Halt with the 3.21 p.m. from Maidstone. In this instance, the train has been strengthened to accommodate the substantial increase in passengers which always occurred during the hop-picking season. The halt has now been upgraded to a station and is simply called Beltring. Teston Crossing Halt, on the other hand, closed in November 1959.

Plate 58: With the early morning mist still lingering, a Tonbridge-bound freight train rounds the curve, just before East Farleigh, on 6th April 1960. The C class engine is in appalling condition, with steam emerging from various parts, contributing to the poor visibility. Neither the cabside number nor the smokebox door number are discernible, but the engine is No. 31590 of Tonbridge Shed.

Plate 59: Maidstone West, where the electric and steam services connected. Two bays were provided for Paddock Wood trains, with the London services using the inner faces of these platforms. Class H, No. 31517, is ready to leave with the 11.46 a.m. to Tonbridge on 4th February 1958. The stock is ex-LBSCR, which was rebuilt for push-pull use by the Southern Railway.

Plate 60: Also from Paddock Wood was a line running south, which was built by the SER. This was the Hawkhurst branch, originally planned to reach Hythe, near Folkestone, by way of Tenterden. In fact, it did not even reach Hawkhurst, as the terminus was over 1½ miles short of the village. The line was opened as far as Goudhurst, in 1892, and to Hawkhurst a year later. There were also stations at Horsmonden and Cranbrook, but all stations except Horsmonden were some way from their respective villages. After opening, the plans were changed, to extend the line to Appledore, again via Tenterden, but this was abandoned by 1899. The branch was push-pull operated, with old ex-LBSCR coaches and the usual Class H tank engine. Traffic was always light, and it was not uncommon to be the only passenger. The only time the line saw much activity was, of course, during the hop-picking season, when longer trains were run during the week and a Sunday service was in operation. Some hop-pickers' specials ran from London, whilst others started either at Tonbridge or Paddock Wood. The problem with using one of these trains for the non hop-picking passenger was that after an early arrival at Hawkhurst, there was no return working until late afternoon. There was ample time to walk to the village and back, but not a great deal of use on a Sunday when the village shop was closed. The author was in this predicament on one occasion, but the problem was solved by the offer of a footplate ride back to Paddock Wood. A journey on a light Class C engine, running tender first was quite an experience. The 1960 hop-picking season found Class C, No. 31244 on Hawkhurst duties, and No. 31693 bound for Maidstone. Both trains are seen at Paddock Wood.

PADDOCK WOOD TO HAWKHURST

Plate 61: Class C, No. 31244, which was shedded at Tonbridge, was often found with the daily Hawkhurst freight train. It is seen at Paddock Wood on 20th August 1959, on its return trip. The engine is about to take water from the SECR water column.

Plate 62: Some idea of the anticipated traffic can be gauged from the size of the stations but, in 1961, just before closure, the afternoon train only provided three passengers for Goudhurst. Although the station house was built of brick, the public part of the station was, from the outset, constructed in corrugated iron, which always looks so ugly, particularly in a country setting.

CLOSURE OF HAWKHURST BRANCH RAILWAY LINE

· ·

On and from MONDAY, 12th JUNE 1961, all services will be withdrawn from the Hawkhurst branch line and HORSMONDEN, GOUDHURST, CRANBROOK and HAWKHURST stations, also Churn Lane and Pattenden sidings, closed.

British Railways will continue to provide collection and delivery services for parcels and freight sundries throughout the area and facilities for truck load traffic exist at other stations in the vicinity.

Further information may be obtained from the Station Master at PADDOCK WOOD (Telephone: 322) or TONBRIDGE (Telephone: 2266) or from the Line Traffic Manager, Southern Region, British Railways, South Eastern Division, 61 Queen Street, London, E.C.4. (Telephone: WATerloo 5151, Ext. 227).

Enquiries in regard to bus services in the area should be addressed to :-

The Maidstone & District Motor Services Ltd.

Knightrider House, Maidstone	-	-	Telephone: 2211
St. John's Road, Tunbridge Wells	-	,,	20221
Opera House Buildings, Tunbridge Wells	-	,,	1700
Sandhurst Road, Hawkhurst	-	- ,,	3169

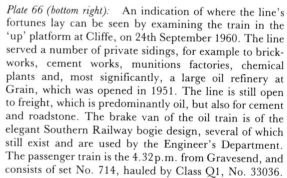

Plate 63: The closure notice, to take effect from 12th June 1961, for all traffic. The bad news is most specific, that the named stations will close. The rest of the information is rather vague. It merely refers to parcels and freight facilities 'throughout the area' and to buses, about which further enquiries to another body should be made.

Plate 65 (top right): Desolate and unattractive areas of Kent seemed to draw the railway companies no less enthusiastically than centres of population, where at least before the advent of the motor car, passengers were guaranteed. One such area was Romney Marsh, and another the Isle of Sheppey. The longest branch, by ½ mile, was, however, that to Port Victoria on the Isle of Grain, which, from its junction with the North Kent line at Hoo, was 11½ miles long. At least that was the case until 1916, when Port Victoria Station, which was on a pier, was declared unsafe. The new terminus, at the landward end of the pier, shortened the branch by a few yards. In 1931, the station was again moved, this time completely on to terra firma. The SER had an interest in the building of the line, as the directors saw a railway from London to the Isle of Grain being able to compete with the LCDR on Sheppey for cross-Channel traffic. In the event, patronage of both Queenborough on Sheppey, and Port Victoria on Grain was poor, although services to a number of North European ports operated for some years. The line was opened initially, in 1882, to Sharnal Street, with one intermediate station at Cliffe. Sharnal Street to Port Victoria was opened five months later, with no intermediate stations. The LCDR had opened Queenborough Pier Station six years previously. From the opening, the majority of trains to Port Victoria started from Gravesend, and continued to do so right up to the end of passenger services in December 1961. There were, however, some through trains from London in the summer months. Trains were frequently, but not exclusively, push-pull operated and Class H, No. 31512 is seen at Gravesend ready to propel the 6.07 p.m. on to the branch, on 24th September 1960.

Plate 66 (bottom right): An indication of where the line's fortunes lay can be seen by examining the train in the 'up' platform at Cliffe, on 24th September 1960. The line served a number of private sidings, for example to brickworks, cement works, munitions factories, chemical plants and, most significantly, a large oil refinery at Grain, which was opened in 1951. The line is still open to freight, which is predominantly oil, but also for cement and roadstone. The brake van of the oil train is of the elegant Southern Railway bogie design, several of which still exist and are used by the Engineer's Department. The passenger train is the 4.32 p.m. from Gravesend, and consists of set No. 714, hauled by Class Q1, No. 33036.

Plate 64 (left): There being no Sunday service, a special was run over the branch on the day following closure. The train had originated in London, and run to Paddock Wood, via Maidstone, behind two SECR 4-4-0s. For the branch trip, a Class 01 and a C class, Nos. 31065 and 31592 were used. They are seen leaving Cranbrook in a shower of rain on the way to Hawkhurst. Their arrival at Hawkhurst was greeted with torrential rain. The train continued to Robertsbridge via Tonbridge, for a visit to the KESR, before returning to London on the Hastings main line (see Plate 48).

Plate 67:   After the formation of the SECR, there was no longer any point in trying to attract European traffic to both Port Victoria and Queenborough. The SECR seriously considered closing Port Victoria altogether, cutting the passenger service back to Sharnal Street. However, destruction of Queenborough by fire, in 1900, necessitated the use of Port Victoria again, and it continued to have boat trains from London for the Continent until 1904. Class H, No. 31530, is seen leaving Sharnal Street with the 2.24p.m. from Allhallows on 2nd December 1961, the last day of passenger services.

Plate 68 (top right):   Halts were added to the line in 1906, at Uralite, near Hoo Junction, at High Halstow, Beluncle, Middle Stoke and Grain Crossing. With passenger traffic dwindling to negligible amounts, Port Victoria and Grain Crossing Halt were closed in 1951, resulting in the line becoming a little shorter for the third time in its history. A new station to serve the oil refinery, and known simply as Grain, was opened the same year and was situated about 300 yards from the halt. Trains were run to and from Grain to coincide with changes in shifts of the refinery workforce, and were, therefore, very infrequent. In this photograph, Class Q1, No. 33036 looks out of place, hauling two pre-grouping coaches on the 11.37a.m. Grain to Gravesend service, seen leaving Beluncle Halt on 24th September 1960.

Plate 69 (bottom right):   Stoke Junction Halt was not opened until 1932, two months after a spur to Allhallows-on-Sea was opened. This was only 1¾ miles long, and was intended to attract clientele from London, seeking the developing holiday resort of the same name. Class Q1, No. 33036 enters the halt with the 3.38p.m. from Allhallows to Gravesend, on 24th September 1960. In the background can be seen the oil refinery at Grain.

DUNTON GREEN TO WESTERHAM

Plate 71 (below): The Westerham branch, which was opened in 1881, left the new SER main line to Dover at Dunton Green, which is just north of Sevenoaks. Although the line pointed ominously toward LBSCR territory, it did not, in reality, offer a threat, as terrain west of Westerham precluded building of a railway other than with substantial engineering works. Therefore, the line was, from the outset, nothing more than a branch with purely local traffic in mind. Dunton Green was only 20½ miles from Charing Cross, and the branch itself was 4¾ miles long. There was one intermediate station, at Brasted, which was conveniently near the village of the same name. The terminus at Westerham was even better placed, in contrast to the situation so often seen on rural railways. In 1906, a halt was opened at Chevening, and at the same time a rail motor service was introduced. The rail motor operation did not last for long, and thereafter a push-pull service was run. There were plans, by the SECR, to electrify the line, but even when electrification by the Southern Railway to Sevenoaks became a reality in 1935, the branch was excluded. It remained steam-operated up to the day of closure. On 24th September 1958, Class H, No. 31177 is seen near Chevening Halt with the 2.20p.m. from Westerham. The stock is interesting, in that both the coaches were originally built, for the SECR, as rail motors. They were abandoned by the end of World War I, but later taken into Southern Railway stock, and converted to conventional carriages. They were formed into set No. 482, and transferred to the Isle of Wight. They returned to the mainland in 1927, and were converted to push-pull operation. They spent the remainder of their existence still as set No. 482 on the Allhallows and Westerham branches. There were, in all, eight SECR rail motors, the remainder also being converted to ordinary coaches by the Southern Railway.

Plate 72 (right): Westerham once had a small engine shed, but this was demolished many years ago. Coaling and watering facilities adjoining the site of the shed were maintained to the end. Class H, No. 31519 is seen taking water on 30th July 1960. The shed site is to the right of the photograph. The antiquated siding signal is worthy of note.

Plate 73: On the afternoon of 28th October 1961, the penultimate day of services, the push-pull train was displaced by a main line train which had come down from London. This train is seen entering the branch at Dunton Green, prior to its first journey to Westerham. The engine is Class D1, No. 31739. For the rest of the day, trains were worked alternately by this engine and a Class Q1 locomotive. Access to the branch was from the 'up' line and the special, therefore, had to reverse over the trailing crossover on arrival at Dunton Green. Because the signal box was on the 'down' main line, a separate tablet instrument was installed on the branch platform, to avoid staff having to continually cross the main line.

Plate 74: There was a joint LBSCR/SER line from London to Oxted. Just south of Oxted, at Hurst Green Junction, one line went to East Grinstead, and was joint as far as Crowhurst Junction, and the other, which was LBSCR, passed through Edenbridge to Tunbridge Wells. The latter route crossed the county boundary from Surrey into Kent, immediately before entering a tunnel over which the SER Tonbridge to Redhill line crossed. Further south, beyond Cowden, the line crossed into Sussex, then back into Kent before reaching the next station of Ashurst. But this was not the end, as the next station, Groombridge, was in Sussex and the terminus at Tunbridge Wells was in Kent. The section from Hurst Green Junction to Edenbridge was opened in 1888. Edenbridge travellers were thus in the enviable position of having two stations, the other on the SER line. Both companies offered a service to London, both via Oxted, the SER reaching Oxted via Crowhurst Junction. In 1896, the LBSCR station was renamed Edenbridge Town, a name which has been retained ever since. Edenbridge Town has also retained its direct service to London, although only at peak times. On 14th April 1960. 'West Country' class No. 34009 *Lyme Regis* leaves Edenbridge Town as evening draws in. The train is the 6.10p.m. Victoria to Brighton, and runs via Eridge and Lewes.

OXTED TO TUNBRIDGE WELLS WEST

Plate 75: Motor trains were introduced in 1907, and halts at Hurst Green and Monks Lane were opened at the same time. Hurst Green Halt was replaced by a new station, nearby, in 1961. Monks Lane Halt was closed in 1939. Another halt, known as High Rocks, between Groombridge and Tunbridge Wells, survived until 1952. A regular push-pull service was run right up to the advent of diesels and set No. 659 was used on 19th May 1961 on the 2.04p.m. Oxted to Tunbridge Wells West train. The engine is Class H, No. 31279 and the train is at Edenbridge Town. The coaches are ex-SECR, which were built as main line stock. The birdcage coach, next to the engine, was built in 1909. These were converted for push-pull operation during 1939, and were used on the Oxted services almost continually, until withdrawal in 1961.

Plate 76: The line beyond Edenbridge Town was opened nine months after the opening of the northern section, and joined the line from East Grinstead to Tunbridge Wells at Ashurst Junction. This line had opened 22 years earlier. South of Edenbridge, there were stations at Hever, Cowden and Ashurst, all very picturesque and in delightful country surroundings. All three stations are still open. There was one tunnel, at the London end of Cowden, which the midday train from Tunbridge Wells West is about to enter, on 2nd September 1961. The train consists of Class H, No. 31543 and set No. 656.

Plate 79: The 4.04 p.m. push-pull train from Oxted is waiting to leave Ashurst, on 23rd March 1961, with Class H, No. 31161. Ashurst was the last station before the junction for Eridge, from which there were trains to both Brighton and Eastbourne. From 1914, through trains from the Oxted line, to both these resorts, were run and coaches were slipped at Ashurst for Tunbridge Wells. Although the slip coaches were withdrawn after the Grouping, up to the introduction of the diesel units, there was one train which split at Ashurst for Tunbridge Wells and Brighton. Just under the station canopy can be seen a fence, behind which is a small lever frame. After the Grouping, several of the smaller stations in the area had their signal boxes dismantled, and the frames resited on the platforms.

Plate 80: The 4.00 p.m. train from Tunbridge Wells West has just negotiated Ashurst Junction, en route to Oxted on 2nd September 1961. The engine is Class H, No. 31278 with the birdcage set, No 659. Although a train of seemingly little importance, it formed part of an integrated pattern of services introduced by British Railways in 1956. Throughout the day, a train left Victoria at eight minutes past each hour for Tunbridge Wells, via Oxted and East Grinstead. At Oxted, it connected with the local train for the Edenbridge line. This left immediately behind the train from London, but, arrived at Tunbridge Wells West 20 minutes earlier. The process was reversed in the 'up' direction.

Plate 81: One of the through trains from Victoria to Brighton and Eastbourne is seen near Ashurst, on 23rd March 1961. The train left London at 3.50p.m. and split at Eridge, where another engine would be waiting to take the rear half to Eastbourne. The engine from London is BR Standard Class 4MT No. 75070, which was designed at Brighton in 1950.

Plate 82: A Victoria-bound train from Tunbridge Wells is pictured at East Grinstead on 7th August 1956. At East Grinstead the 'up' and 'down' trains passed, as there was only a single line between Ashurst Junction and East Grinstead. These trains also connected with the service which ran between East Grinstead and Three Bridges. In fact, this offered an alternative way to London, as at Three Bridges there was a connection with the electric trains to London. This LMSR Class 4MT, No. 42087, was built at Brighton in 1950. Many of this class were used on the Sussex lines until the advent of BR Standard tank engines, again mostly Brighton-built or designed.

Plate 83 (top right): Groombridge was another important station in the BR fixed interval services of East Sussex. The direct trains to and from Oxted connected here with those for Brighton and Eastbourne. The former originated from Tonbridge, and the latter from Tunbridge Wells West. They arrived at Groombridge within a few minutes of each other. Similarly efficient connections applied in the reverse direction. On 16th March 1958, Class 4MT No. 42089, with the 11.47a.m. working from Tunbridge Wells West to Victoria, passes the late-running 'down' train at Groombridge. Due to the complicated nature of the services, delays at one point would throw the system into chaos, which would either result in lost connections, or late running throughout the system. The other difficulty was that passengers had to acquaint themselves with any necessary changes, in order to gain maximum benefit from the linked services. For most of the day it was, for example, necessary for travellers from London to change both at Oxted and Groombridge for the stations on the Brighton and Eastbourne lines. Despite this, the service was, for the most part, excellent, and it is to be regretted that the closures, which took place in the 1960s, included much of this part of the network.

Plate 84 (bottom right): A few trains between Tunbridge Wells and London took the direct route through Edenbridge, and one of these is seen leaving Groombridge behind Standard 4MT No. 80033, on 2nd September 1961. In common with most of the others in rural Sussex, Groombridge station was very well maintained, and even had some sizeable flower beds, seen in the foreground. The station re-opened in 1996 and a service is run by the Spa Valley Railway to Tunbridge Wells West.

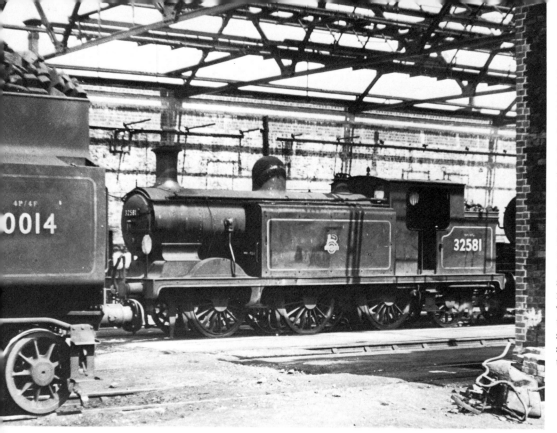

Plate 85: Tunbridge Wells West Engine Shed, shown in this photograph without a roof, was reconstructed in the late 1950s. This was the second shed at Tunbridge Wells, and replaced an earlier one in 1890. The majority of the allocation was for passenger work and, until the introduction by British Railways of Standard tank engines, was a miscellaneous collection of pre-grouping engines which included Class E4 0-6-2Ts, Class D3 0-4-4Ts and larger tank engines of the LBSCR. When the latter were withdrawn, the services to the coast were operated mainly be SECR 4-4-0s. The D3s were replaced by SECR H class tanks. Class E4 No. 32581 was on shed on 1st September 1955. The shed is now the headquarters of the Spa Valley Railway.

Plate 86: The railway from Groombridge Station to Groombridge Junction was in an attractively wooded cutting, and was a most pleasant place to spend a day. With four trains an hour, in each direction, there was little time for rest. On 16th March 1958 one of the 2-6-4Ts of BR, No. 80147, recently allocated to Tunbridge Wells West Shed, runs bunker first towards Groombridge with the 10.45a.m. from Eastbourne. The coaches form set No. 945, built for the Hastings line in 1932, and are only 8ft. 0¾in. wide. There were several such sets, each consisting of two brake composite coaches between which was an all-third. They were known as 'O' sets.

Plate 87: Groombridge Junction signal box was in the 'vee' of the junction itself, across which ran a well-positioned footbridge. Approaching the junction from Groombridge, on 16th March 1958, is a Brighton train hauled by Class L1, No. 31787. The train is the 12.10 p.m. from Tonbridge, and reaches the ex-LBSCR system by a short single line interconnecting Tunbridge Wells Central and Tunbridge Wells West. This line, which was one of the most heavily occupied lengths of single track in the country, passes through Grove Tunnel. This is of narrow bore, but will accommodate both Restriction 0 and Restriction 1 (i.e. 8 ft. 6½ in. wide) stock. On this occasion, a 4 coach set, No. 425 is used. The coaches originally formed part of a 7 coach set, built for the Kent Coast express trains in 1924. They were formed into the present set in 1928, and continued to be used on London to Ramsgate services until about 1956.

Plate 88: On the same day, an 'up' train from Brighton crosses Groombridge Junction, with Class D1, No. 31470 of Tonbridge. From the beginning of 1959, the signal boxes at Groombridge, Ashurst and Birchden junctions were all closed, and the triangle was controlled from a new box at Groombridge Station.

Plate 89: The Eastbourne and Brighton lines diverged one mile south of Eridge, at Redgate Mill Junction. The first station on the Eastbourne line proper was Rotherfield & Mark Cross. The line was single throughout, and formed an extension of the short Hailsham branch near Eastbourne. A glance at the Ordnance Survey map shows the line to be severely graded, with numerous sharp curves, even through the stations. There were two tunnels, one between Rotherfield and Mayfield, and the other at Heathfield. In late British Railways' days at least, trains were usually composed of only two coaches, and were almost invariably hauled by BR Standard 2-6-4Ts. No. 80095 drifts into Rotherfield & Mark Cross on a wet day in March 1961 with the 1.39 p.m. from Tunbridge Wells West to Eastbourne.

Plate 90: The bunker of a BR tank engine seems even more massive when viewed at a low angle. No. 80084 is seen with the 10.39a.m. from Tunbridge Wells West at Rotherfield & Mark Cross on 16th August 1962. Diesels arrived on the line the same year, but by then, patronage at all the stations north of Hailsham was low. The line was closed completely between Redgate Mill Junction and Hailsham, at the beginning of the summer timetable in 1965.

Plate 91: On 29th March 1961, the Eastbourne-bound freight train emerges from Heathfield Tunnel. This train shunts at all stations en route as required, but always at Heathfield which had the largest yard. Hellingly, two stations further south, had a private railway running to a nearby hospital. There was an interchange siding, at which the 'down' goods would often shunt, although the private line was closed at the end of the 1950s. The extraordinary thing about this line is that it was electrically-operated, with an overhead tramcar-type pick-up. On this occasion the engine is Class C, No. 31244.

Plate 92: Hailsham was the largest town on the line, and the station was centrally-placed. In addition to the hourly service, there were trains from Eastbourne and Polegate which terminated at Hailsham. On 13th April 1962, Standard Class 4MT, No. 80150 with the 12.39p.m. train from Tunbridge Wells West, enters Hailsham. In the 'up' platform is an ex-LBSCR Class E4, No. 32470, which had earlier worked a train from Eastbourne with set No. 609. By this time, E4s were rarely seen on passenger trains, as most had been withdrawn. This particular engine was withdrawn two months later.

Plate 93: Between trips, the local service engine would engage in shunting in Hailsham Yard. In this view, Class E4, No. 32470 prepares to pick up some vans for transfer to Polegate.

Plate 94: Another Hailsham train, this time running only as far as Polegate, to collect returning commuters from London, on the evening of 13th April 1962. The 3 coach train is hauled by ex-LBSCR Class K, No. 32347. The steam service was replaced by diesel units, and the service to Hailsham continued until 1968.

Plate 95: Eastbourne's first station opened in 1849, at the end of a spur from the Brighton to Hastings line. The station was resited in 1886, and rebuilt at the time of the electrification in 1935. For the new service to London a number of 6 car corridor sets were built, differing from the later Portsmouth electric stock, in that there was no corridor connection at each end of the set. Trains were usually formed of two or three sets, which were therefore isolated from each other. For stopping trains, 2 coach units, which were converted from old LSWR coaches, and some newly-built units, were used. The wartime-designed units, known as '2HALs' were also used, but although more modern, were rather uncomfortable. On 13th April 1962, '2HAL' No. 2657 prepares to leave on the coastal service. The normal pattern of services along the coast, at this time, was a half-hourly 'all stations' train between Brighton and Ore. All trains called at Eastbourne, necessitating reversal after a three minute stop. The main line trains also started from Ore, and took just under 1½ hours from Eastbourne to Victoria. Few trains used the direct coast line, avoiding Eastbourne. An E4, No. 32470 is waiting to take vans to Hailsham, and is hiding behind the electric unit.

Plate 96: When the line from Polegate to Hastings was first opened, there was no direct connection into Eastbourne from the Hastings direction. A spur was subsequently added at Stone Cross, and between here and Bexhill, there was only one intermediate station, at Pevensey. In 1905, five halts were added, although one located at Collington Wood was closed during the following year. In 1911, a new halt was opened on the same site and was called West Bexhill, but this was renamed Collington Halt in 1929. Apart from being rebuilt by the Southern Railway and losing the suffix 'halt' a few years ago, it has remained unchanged. On 14th August 1956, two '4LAV' units, Nos. 2950 and 2953, pass Collington Halt with a Victoria to Ore train. These units were built by the Southern Railway at Lancing and Eastleigh in 1931/2, for semi-fast work in Sussex. Three out of the four coaches in each unit were non-corridor vehicles.

Plate 97: Eridge, in common with several other stations in Sussex, had a train service far more intense than the local traffic required, by virtue of its position as a railway junction. The first railway to reach Eridge was that from Lewes, and it was opened in 1868. When the Eastbourne line was first opened, the two lines which ran parallel from Redgate Mill to Eridge, were worked as independent single tracks. Redgate Mill Junction was installed in 1894, from which time conventional 'up' and 'down' working commenced. This change took place at the same time as the doubling of the Lewes line as far as Uckfield. South of Uckfield, the line was already double. A heavily overcast day in March 1961 found Class U1, No. 31906 with the 9.55a.m. Brighton to Victoria train leaving Eridge.

TONBRIDGE TO BRIGHTON

Plate 98: The 'down' service, also at Eridge, in the hands of Standard Class 4MT, No. 80067, had left Victoria at 10.38a.m. These London trains did not, of course call at Groombridge, but took the spur which linked Eridge with Ashurst. The 'down' train also consists of through coaches for Eastbourne, and these are detached at Eridge. They are taken forward on the rear of the Tonbridge to Eastbourne train, which can be seen in the bay on the right.

Plate 100 (top right): On 27th March 1961, Standard Class 4MT, No. 80153 is pictured with the 5.10p.m. working from Tonbridge. There were severe shortages of narrow-bodied stock, as a result of the policy of the time to condemn all coaches over a certain age, irrespective of their condition. It was, therefore, sometimes necessary to cut the Brighton service back to Tunbridge Wells West, with little warning to potential passengers. The train is seen just beyond Crowborough, which is situated 40 miles from London. The mile post signifies that the point is 23 miles from Brighton, in keeping with the fact that the line was constructed from south to north.

Plate 101 (bottom right): Emerging from Crowborough Tunnel on 27th March 1961 is Class N1, No. 31822 with the 3.55p.m. from Brighton to Tonbridge. The line climbs continuously for three miles at gradients of 1 in 75 and 1 in 80, until reaching this point. The N1 locomotive could be distinguished from the N class more by its beat than by its appearance, as it was a three cylinder engine. The length of Crowborough Tunnel is 1,022 yards. The other major engineering works on the line are two masonry viaducts, between Buxted and Crowborough.

Plate 99: The Tonbridge to Brighton services were usually in the hands of Maunsell Moguls until the advent of diesel power. On 27th March 1961, the 'up' 2.55p.m. ex-Brighton and the 'down' 3.10p.m. ex-Tonbridge trains pass at Crowborough, with Class U1, No. 31892 with the 'down' train. The station was originally called Rotherfield, but on the opening of a station to serve Rotherfield on the Eastbourne line, the name was changed to Crowborough. In 1887, the railways, presumably realizing that there was a nearer village to the station than Crowborough, altered the name to Crowborough & Jarvis Brook. After closure south of Uckfield, the name again reverted to Crowborough.

Plate 102: South of Uckfield, the line ran through flatter country, and at Isfield, it met the River Ouse, which it followed into Lewes. The area around Barcombe Mills Station was subject to flooding. Class N, No. 31861 is captured on a pleasant spring afternoon in 1961, leaving Barcombe Mills for Tonbridge. Just south of Barcombe Mills was Culver Junction, where the line from East Grinstead was met. Until this line was opened, with its own station at Barcombe, Barcombe Mills was, itself, called Barcombe.

Plate 103: At Lewes, the steam-operated services from Tonbridge and East Grinstead met up with electric trains on the South Coast line, and with the expresses from London. A most inappropriate formation for a 'Brighton' section train is seen at Lewes on 7th August 1958. The engine is SECR Class L, No. 31761 and the coaches consist of a birdcage 3 set, also of SECR origin. This forms the 2.02 p.m. from Brighton to Tunbridge Wells West. It is odd that the SECR never penetrated LBSCR territory to this extent in pre-grouping days, but by early British Railways' times, it was commonplace.

Plate 104 (above): Lewes Station, viewed from a road bridge, shows Class N, No. 31403 with the 7 a.m. Swansea to Eastbourne train, and '2HAL' electric unit No. 2625 on the Ore to Brighton service. Through trains from other regions were regular visitors in the summer months. Although usually hauled by Southern motive power, they used the home region's stock. The first station at Lewes opened in 1846, as part of the Brighton to Hastings line. The direct line from London reached Lewes the following year. In the south, a line to Newhaven Harbour was also constructed, and was later extended to Seaford. A new station was opened at Lewes in 1857. The line as far as Uckfield followed in 1859, from a junction north of the new station on the London line. This entailed a reversal of all trains running between Uckfield and Brighton. However, once the Uckfield line was extended to Tunbridge Wells, the approach to Lewes was resited. A connection was made east of the station, to enable direct running on to Brighton. Because of the cramped and busy nature of the station, a goods avoiding line was built, from which there was access to extensive marshalling yards. Lewes was included in the 1935 electrification programme.

Plate 105 (below): Newhaven was an important railway centre, by virtue of the harbour which saw regular boat trains, hauled, for many years, by Marsh Atlantics and later by the Bulleid-Raworth electric locomotives. Newhaven was also host to more macabre activities, namely the gutting of hundreds of woodenbodied coaches. On 22nd April 1961, Class C, No. 31280 shunts the remains of some coaches into the yard, at Newhaven Town *(see also Plate 123).*

Plate 106: A railway was constructed to connect Lewes with East Grinstead in 1882. At this time, there was no rail connection north to Oxted and London, although such a line was built two years later *(see Plate 74)*. There were six intermediate stations, two tunnels and one viaduct which was just south of East Grinstead. All the stations were substantially built in anticipation of traffic which really did not exist, as the line served only villages en route. The line was double from East Grinstead to Horsted Keynes, and single thereafter. It entered Lewes by joining the Tunbridge Wells to Lewes line at Culver Junction. This photograph shows one of the stations, West Hoathly, in May 1955.

Plate 107: Most trains only ran between East Grinstead and Brighton, although there were a few through workings from London, even in British Railways times. On Sundays, the only two trains of the day were through trains. Closure of the line was announced for the beginning of the summer timetable in 1955, but took place, by default, on 29th May, because of a rail strike. However, it had to be reopened the following year because it appeared that an Act of Parliament was necessary to make closure legal. The first day of the reinstated service found Class C2X No. 32442 and ex-LBSCR set No. 504 approaching East Grinstead. The new service was two-hourly, and ran only between East Grinstead and Lewes. Trains omitted to stop at Kingscote and Barcombe throughout the period of reopening, because neither station was mentioned in the original Act. It could be said that British Railways did not exactly operate the service with enthusiasm.

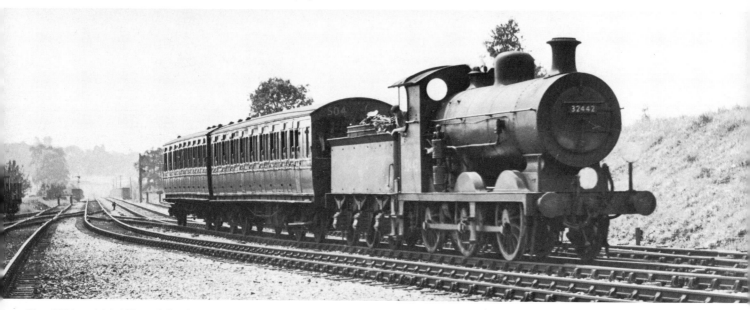

Plate 108 (top right): Although local support of the line was vigorous in spirit, it was not numerically large and most trains were run with just a single coach. On 18th February 1958, Standard Class 4MT No. 80150 works the 1.30p.m. from Lewes, with ex-LBSCR brake third No.3847, at West Hoathly.

Plate 109 (bottom right): The second, and presumably final, closure was fixed for 17th March 1958. The last train was the 4.28p.m. East Grinstead to Lewes, and this was formed of several corridor coaches, packed with passengers and hauled by Standard Class 4MT No. 80154. It is seen, complete with a drooping bluebell on the smokebox door, at Newick & Chailey. Although Newick & Chailey did indeed close, and the station area was subsequently swallowed up by a housing development, the line north of Horsted Keynes is well and truly open, as the Bluebell Railway.

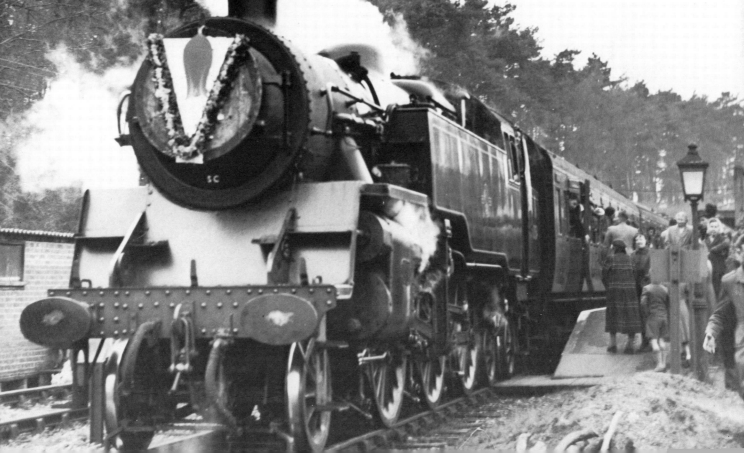

Plate 110: The main intermediate station was Horsted Keynes, where there was a branch to the London to Brighton line, at Copyhold. There was no junction at Copyhold until 1931. Prior to this, trains ran on an independent line which was parallel with the main line into Haywards Heath. Even after closure to regular services, occasional trains were run from London to East Grinstead, and on to the northern part of the line to Horsted Keynes. On 11th May 1958, Class K, No. 32342 leaves Horsted Keynes for Haywards Heath with a special train.

Plate 111: The northern section of the line from East Grinstead, was to have been electrified by the Southern Railway, thus giving an alternative route from London to Haywards Heath and Brighton. In the event, the only part to be electrified was from Horsted Keynes to Copyhold Junction. The availability of an alternative route was one of the arguments used against closure of the line, as there had, over the years, been a number of occasions when trains had been re-routed via Horsted Keynes, due to blockages on the main line. A passenger service continued between Horsted Keynes and Haywards Heath and on to Seaford, until 1963. After that, a goods only service was retained from Haywards Heath to Ardingly, the only intermediate station. Between Ardingly and Horsted Keynes was a high and imposing viaduct, which has now been demolished. On 21st October 1962, '2HAL' electric unit, No. 2657 stops at Ardingly with a train for Horsted Keynes.

Plate 112: The first railway to East Grinstead was built in 1885, from Three Bridges on the London to Brighton main line. There was one intermediate station, at Rowfant, and another was added five years later at Grange Road. This may account for the contrasting styles of the two buildings. The line was 6¾ miles long, and ran through pleasant wooded countryside for most of the way. It was single track throughout, other than a passing loop at Rowfant. Although, for most of its existence, the line was operated in isolation from the rest of the network, there was, at one time, a slip coach for East Grinstead which was dropped at Horley from an evening London to Brighton train. The line has always had a frequent service, and was reasonably well patronized. It was somewhat surprising that it was closed at the beginning of 1967. On 2nd May 1958, the service is being worked by Class M7, No. 30109 and a push-pull set, No. 758, consisting of ex-LBSCR coaches, which are seen approaching East Grinstead.

Plate 113: On the same day, Class H, No.31554 hauls the 9.45 a.m. Three Bridges to East Grinstead train also with a set of ex-LBSCR coaches. It is a pity that there were no 'Brighton' engines available to work the line. The train is leaving Grange Road, which, in 1958, had only just run out of its last remaining stock of LBSCR tickets, but still had Southern Railway tickets to several destinations.

EAST GRINSTEAD TO THREE BRIDGES

Plate 114: Some years later, on 9th September 1961, H class tanks were still in use, and No. 31551 waits to leave Rowfant with the 1.08 p.m. from Three Bridges. The old 'Brighton' coaching stock has, however, long since been condemned, and all trains are composed of the BR push-pull rebuilds of Maunsell corridor stock, in this instance set No.606.

Plate 115: From Grange Road, the line descends at an incline of 1 in 80 to Rowfant. The descent can clearly be seen in the photograph, and the line drops further before levelling out at Three Bridges. Rowfant was built mainly to serve the nearby Rowfant House, which is reached by way of the level crossing in front of the station. In the station is Class H, No. 31551, propelling a train to East Grinstead.

Plate 116 (right): Although the C2X class 0-6-0s were often seen on the daily freight train, they were not used on regular passenger trains over the branch. However, they were employed on occasional specials, such as this one, in September 1961, showing No. 32523. This train had run from Forest Row, and was heading for North Camp on the Guildford to Reading line. The signal in the foreground is a standard LSWR pattern lattice post, but with a British Railways' arm. LBSCR signals were rare, because the 'Brighton' used wooden posts, most of which had been replaced by the Southern Railway.

Plate 117 (previous page): On 3rd June 1960, Class M7, No. 30055 with Maunsell set No. 602 is seen with the 12.27p.m. from East Grinstead, in the woods, just before the Brighton main line comes into view at Three Bridges.

Plate 118: A departure from Three Bridges on 7th October 1962, by Class H, No. 31544 with the 10.27a.m. to East Grinstead. In the background is the main line, and the modern Three Bridges signal box.

Plate 119: There was an early morning freight train to Rowfant, consisting of oil tankers, and if there were no return empties, the engine would be attached to the first convenient passenger train, which would then run double-headed back to Three Bridges. Such was the case on 21st May 1958, when the 9a.m. from East Grinstead entered Three Bridges behind Class M7, No. 30109 and Class H, No. 31554. It was normal, after allowing passengers to disembark, to shunt the train to the end of the platform so that the engine could take water.

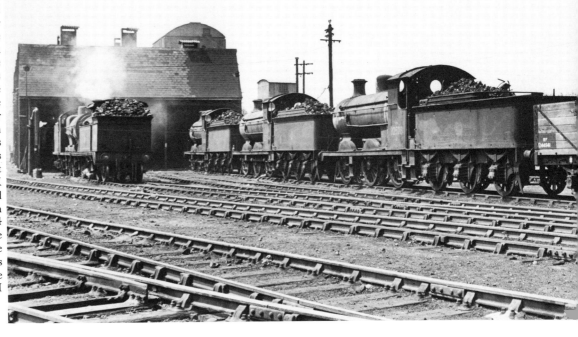

Plate 120: The original Three Bridges Engine Shed was built in the 'vee' of the Brighton and Horsham lines. A much larger shed was constructed in the same area, around 1909, complete with a 60 ft. turntable. Much of the allocation was of 'Brighton' goods engines, as there were large marshalling yards nearby. Three Bridges also provided engines for the local passenger trains. Even after the main and Horsham lines were electrified, Three Bridges was still busy. Many of the freight trains were handled by Class C2X engines, several of which could always be found in the vicinity. On 3rd June 1960, Nos. 32528, 32534 and 32535 were lined up outside the shed. There were usually the more modern Class Q locomotives present as well, and one can be seen on the left, behind a Class H tank.

THREE BRIDGES TO BRIGHTON

Plate 121: On 20th February 1956, a snow-bound Class M7, No. 30058 is found resting at the rear of Three Bridges Shed. The 'not to be moved' notice on the smokebox would seem to be superfluous, when it is seen that the engine has no front driving wheels. In the background is the engineer's yard, which was still in use in 1983.

Plate 122: Study of an elegant design. The Billinton Class K, 2-6-0s were used exclusively in Sussex, and many of the class were allocated to Three Bridges. On 7th October 1962, Nos. 32344 in the foreground, and 32343, are outside the shed. The shed was closed two years later, and was eventually demolished.

Plate 123: During the mass withdrawal of pre-grouping coaches in the 1950s, many of these vehicles were stored in sidings and on disused lines in Sussex. Part of the Haywards Heath to Horsted Keynes branch was used, and the branch was then operated as a single line. There were also coaches at Gatwick Airport Station, and in the yards of several other Brighton main line stations. Hassocks was used to store old electric units, and two ex-LSWR coaches are seen there on 9th October 1955. These are motor coaches from '4 SUB' unit, No. 4164.

Plate 124: One of the most famous trains in the world, the 'Brighton Belle', approaches Three Bridges on 7th October 1962. There had been Pullman cars on the London to Brighton line since 1875, but from 1934, it was possible to enjoy the double luxuries of Pullman travel and electric traction. As in steam days, there were also Pullman cars in many of the best London to South Coast trains, but somehow a single brown and cream coach amongst five green coaches always seemed out of place. There were three 'Brighton Belle' units, each consisting of two driving brake third saloons, one third class parlour saloon and two first class kitchen cars. They were built by the Metropolitan-Cammell Carriage, Wagon & Finance Company and were the property of the Pullman Car Company, based at Preston Park just outside Brighton. There had been rumours about withdrawal of the train, around the time this photograph was taken, but eventually British Railways decided to refurbish the units instead. Although this, no doubt, gave them a new lease of life, the attempt to modernize their appearance by, for example, eliminating the Pullman livery, somehow spoilt the effect. The units were withdrawn when the other Southern Railway main line electric stock was replaced by BR units. However, some coaches from the 'Belle' have been privately purchased.

Plate 125: The Brighton main line had been electrified for so many years that, for many people, the sight of steam on the line was only a dream. There were a few steam workings in British Railways' days, mainly of parcels traffic and through workings from other regions, but nothing as extraordinary, as seen on 15th September 1963. A special train had run from British Railways to the Bluebell Railway. The return train from Haywards Heath to Victoria was double-headed by Caledonian Single, No. 123 and LSWR T9, No. 120, seen in attractive surroundings as the sun was setting near the Ouse Valley Viaduct.

Plate 128 (top right): The best view of Brighton Shed was from the road, which climbed steeply along the western side of the station. From here, one could look over the coast line, and obtain a bird's-eye view of the whole shed area. In pre-electric days, the shed had an allocation of over 100 engines., the majority of which were, themselves, ex-LBSCR. Even in the 1950s there were about sixty engines, predominantly 'Brighton' but also the 'King Arthurs', Maunsell Moguls, Qs, Q1s and BR Standard types. Engines were often stored at Brighton Shed, prior to removal to the works, for cutting up. On 7th October 1956, ex-SECR Class D, No. 31549 is awaiting this fate. At this time, the shed also contained all the Marsh Atlantic Class H2 locomotives, which had just been withdrawn. Behind the 4-4-0 is No. 32424 *Beachy Head.* There were rumours for several years afterwards that one of this class had not been cut up, but had been retained inside Brighton Works for preservation. Unfortunately, it was a story never to be substantiated, as when the works site was cleared for a car-park, there was no sign of any remaining engines.

Plate 126 (above): Brighton was not only a holiday resort and cultural centre with the Royal Pavilion, but was also a railway centre. The station, with its massive roof, was one of the historic buildings of the town. Brighton was the headquarters of the LBSCR, and its locomotive works, which was opened in 1852, was situated adjacent to the eastern side of the station. It is just visible in the photograph, although it had been closed for several years. There were extensive sheds for housing electrics and a motive power depot, virtually at the end of the platform, in the 'vee' of the London and Worthing lines. The last regular steam-hauled train from London to Brighton ran in the early hours of New Year's Day, 1933. Since then, Brighton always conjured up a picture of electric units efficiently entering and leaving the station, for destinations along the South Coast and to London. But there was always plenty of steam. From the eastern side of the terminus ran the Tonbridge trains and, from the other side, the push-pull trains to Horsham, all making Brighton a most interesting and active station. On 7th October 1962, Class K, No. 32353 emerges from the station on a special working along the coast.

Plate 129 (bottom right): One of several Class E4 locomotives, allocated to Brighton Shed, is No. 32469, shown hauling a diesel shunter, No. D2282 and a 'West Country' Pacific, in the shed yard on 27th March 1961. The E4s were used for local shunting duties, occasionally on the Horsham trains and on the workmen's train to Lancing Carriage Works. This train, which was usually double-headed and consisted of LSWR coaches, was known locally as the 'Lancing Belle'.

Plate 127 (left): In the summer months, inter-regional trains came mainly from Leicester, Sheffield, Manchester, Walsall, Birmingham and Wolverhampton. Throughout the year, there were trains to Bournemouth West, Plymouth Friary, Chester and Cardiff. The trains from the Western Region were formed on alternate days by Southern and Western rolling stock. For these trains, Brighton Shed had an allocation of Light Pacifics. On 29th March 1962, Class E4, No. 32469 hauls a train of empty stock, from an inter-regional working, out of the station for berthing.

Plate 130: There always seemed to be a Class K pottering around Brighton. On this occasion, 27th March 1961, No. 32337 runs light into the station. These engines were built at Brighton, the first, being the one in the photograph, appearing at the end of 1913. They carried the bulk of heavy freight associated with the war effort on the 'Brighton' lines. After World War I, they were also used on passenger trains, and they performed both these duties admirably, although they were built as goods engines.

Plate 131: Horsham had a small engine shed but, most unusually for the South of England, it was a roundhouse. The shed was quite important in the early days, although the advent of electric trains through Horsham in 1938 obviously reduced its allocation. In British Railways' times, it had a small number of ex-LBSCR engines for local shunting duties for the Midhurst, Guildford and Brighton passenger trains and for goods workings. On 9th October 1955, the shed contained Classes E4, No. 32470. Q, No. 30534, M7, No. 30048 and C2X, No. 32523. The shed was closed in 1964 and the area has been redeveloped.

Plate 132: Between Horsham and Christ's Hospital, both electric and steam trains could be seen, the former on the Mid-Sussex line and the latter on the push-pull services to Guildford and Brighton. At Christ's Hospital, the Guildford line turned sharply west, and the remaining lines diverged, about half a mile further on, at Itchingfield Junction. Christ's Hospital Station was built in the 'vee' of the first junction, so that Guildford trains had their own platform literally at the beginning of the branch. The other lines shared a single 'up' platform, but on the 'down' side there was also a loop. On 24th March 1961, Class E4, No. 32468 leaves Christ's Hospital with the 4.53p.m. Horsham to Guildford train. In the background are the branch platforms.

HORSHAM TO
BRIGHTON

Plate 133: A year previously to the day, Class H, No. 31308 leaves Christ's Hospital with the 9.30a.m. Horsham to Guildford train, making a tremendous effort to move a mere three coaches. The line passed through some pleasant countryside to the village stations of Slinfold and Rudgwick. It then crossed the county boundary into Surrey, where there was somewhat more potential traffic at Cranleigh and Bramley.

Plate 134 (below):   Christ's Hospital was 2¼ miles from Horsham. This view of the junction at Christ's Hospital, shows Class 2MT, No. 41303 and set No. 604 with the 4.19p.m. train to Brighton. The rebuilt Maunsell sets were first used on this line in 1959. The junction itself was known as Stammerham Junction. At one time, it was possible for trains to run direct from Brighton on to the Guildford branch by means of a spur, known as the Itchingfield South Fork. This was opened in 1865, but was closed only two years later. Christ's Hospital Station was opened in 1902.

Plate 135 (top right):   The Horsham to Brighton line was opened in 1861, and doubled 16 years later. The first station on the line was Southwater, which served a village situated on the main road from London to Worthing, now the A24. Class M7, No. 30055 is seen in the open country between Southwater and Itchingfield Junction, with the 2p.m. from Brighton, on 4th March 1958.

Plate 136 (bottom right):   Partridge Green was another attractive country station, which even in British Railways' days, retained many of its 'Brighton' attributes, including the oil lamps, original buildings and the footbridge. Apart from the years immediately before closure, trains were often composed of LBSCR stock and hauled by pre-grouping engines. However, modernization did eventually arrive, and Bulleid main line sets became quite common, and were hauled by Standard tank engines. On 27th July 1963, Bulleid set, No. 92 and Class 2MT, No. 41230 form the 2.21p.m. Horsham to Brighton train. The line closed on 7th March 1966, although the section from Shoreham to Beeding, at the southern end of the line, was kept open for cement traffic.

Plate 137: Steyning was really the only town of any size on the line, as a result of which two trains per day from Brighton terminated there. There were thirteen 'down' and twelve 'up' trains on the branch during the week and, even on Sundays, there were nine trains. Apart from those terminating at Steyning, every train called at all stations on the branch, although one omitted Christ's Hospital, and several left out Southwick and Portslade, which were between Shoreham and Brighton. From just south of Steyning, the line followed the River Adur to Shoreham. It was at Shoreham that the branch joined the Worthing to Brighton electrified line. Class M7 No. 30049 is entering Steyning with the 11.37a.m. from Brighton, on 24th July 1960.

Plate 138: An 'up' vans train passes through Steyning on 24th July 1960. The engine is Standard Class 4MT No. 80067, and the leading vehicle is a Southern Railway bogie guards van. There were 100 of these vehicles, built between 1937 and 1939 for parcels and newspaper traffic. A further 30 were built by British Railways in 1952.

Plate 139 (above): The last few yards of the journey, with an ex-LMSR designed Class 2MT entering Brighton on an afternoon train from Horsham in midsummer 1962. The photograph was taken from the end of the Worthing line platform. On this stretch of line, there were originally five intermediate stations. With the introduction, by the LBSCR, of steam rail motor trains in 1905, five halts were added, thus providing a station, on average, every half a mile. All of the stations and three of the halts are still open, although those at Holland Road and Bungalow Town have closed. Dyke Junction Halt is now called Aldrington, and Ham Bridge Halt is called East Worthing.

Plate 140 (below): The Mid-Sussex line was built as a means of enabling the LBSCR trains to reach Portsmouth from London, without the need to go via Brighton. It was also designed to seal off Sussex from the LSWR. A single line was opened from Horsham to Petworth in 1859. This was doubled as far as Hardham Junction, from which the line was extended to Arundel in 1863. Petworth remained a terminus until 1866, when the line was extended to Midhurst to meet the LSWR line from Petersfield. The two railways had separate stations which were physically connected two months later. The LSWR station was closed in 1925, and trains from both the ex-LBSCR and ex-LSWR lines used the 'Brighton' station. Apart from specials, the two lines had separate services so that, although Midhurst was a through station, it was used as a terminus. A third line, from Chichester, reached Midhurst in 1881, but this was closed to passengers in 1935 *(see Plates 143 and 144)*. The Mid-Sussex line was electrified in 1938, but the Midhurst branches were always steam-operated. The 3.48p.m. to Petersfield waits, at Midhurst on 29th January 1955, to be propelled by Class M7, No. 30028. The line right through from Hardham Junction to Petersfield was closed to passengers a week later. According to the local press, the last train was worked by a 'tank and drum' engine, doubtless a strange shorthand rendering for a Drummond tank!

PULBOROUGH TO MIDHURST

Plate 141 (top right): The Sunday after closure saw a railway enthusiasts' special over the line, double-headed by two Class E5X tank engines. This made a most impressive sight, all the more splendid by the playing of the 'Last Post' by a lone bugler standing on a hill overlooking the railway, just beyond Midhurst. For the next few years, there were summer excursions for ramblers, railway enthusiasts and polo supporters to see the matches at Cowdray Park. One such train was hauled by a Class Q, No. 30549, and it is seen returning to London in evening light at Selham on 8th June 1958.

Plate 142 (bottom right): A reminder of the first Sunday after closure, with two ex-LBSCR tanks, but over seven years later, on 24th June 1962. The engines are Classes E4, No. 32503 and E6, No. 32417 and they are seen passing Selham Station. A few wagons can be seen in the yard. Freight services did not cease until 1964 between Petworth and Midhurst, and from Pulborough to Petworth in 1966.

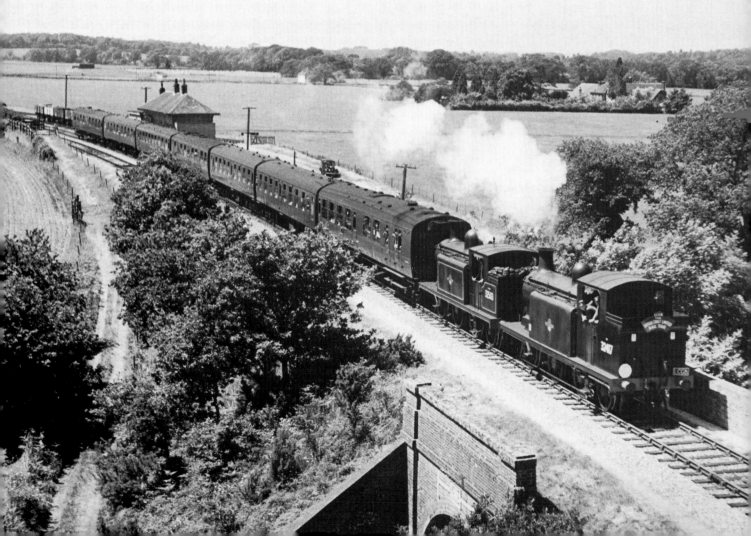

Plate 143 (right): Although the Chichester to Midhurst line was closed to passengers in 1935, the line remained open to freight until 1951 when a train was derailed near Cocking, on a culvert which collapsed. The northern part of the line was never re-opened. However, freight trains continued to run between Chichester and Cocking for some years, until the line was cut back even further, to Lavant. Occasional railway enthusiasts' trains were run on the remains of the branch and, on at least two occasions, there were long double-headed trains of corridor stock. One of these events took place on 3rd November 1963 when the train was hauled by Class Q locomotives Nos. 30531 and 30543. It is seen here near Fishbourne, which is just west of the junction for Lavant. The line was closed to all traffic in 1968, then re-opened in 1972 for gravel trains, but has since completely closed again.

CHICHESTER TO MIDHURST

Plate 144 (below): On 7th March 1959, a special tour of Hampshire and West Sussex lines included Lavant in its itinerary. The engine, Class M7 No. 30111, is seen taking water at Chichester during the first part of the tour which had started from Portsmouth Harbour. Chichester had the unenviable reputation of being the most decrepit of all Southern Region stations, which even provoked correspondence in national newspapers. It was rebuilt in 1958.

INDEX OF LOCATIONS